The ISO/TS 16949 Answer Book

The ISO/TS 16949 Answer Book

A Step-By-Step Guide for Automotive Suppliers

Radley M. Smith
Roderick A. Munro
Ronald J. Bowen

Paton Press LLC • Chico, California

Most Paton Press books are available at quantity discounts when purchased in bulk. For more information, contact:

Paton Press LLC
PO Box 44
Chico, CA 95927-0044
Telephone: (530) 342-5480
Fax: (530) 342-5471
E-mail: *books@patonpress.com*
Web: *www.patonpress.com*

Staff
Publisher ....Scott M. Paton
Editor ....Finn Kraemer
Book Design ....Caylen Balmain

Contents

Preface

The response to *The QS-9000 Answer Book* was both gratifying and encouraging. Thus encouraged, and with the replacement of QS-9000 by ISO/TS 16949 already underway, we hope to provide assistance to anyone seeking to understand ISO/TS 16949:2002 and its application in the automotive supply chain. My goal in writing *The QS-9000 Answer Book* was to de-mystify QS-9000 and make it more understandable. Although my co-authors and I hope to do the same for ISO/TS 16949:2002, we also hope to help automotive suppliers add value as they prepare for registration.

Registration alone does not make a supplier great. However, developing a value-adding quality management system can. Following the process described in this book is a significant step in that direction. I am fortunate to have two experienced co-authors on this project, Rod Munro and Jerry Bowen. They have contributed their experience in various aspects of automotive quality improvement. We hope that you find our efforts helpful.

One caution: In those chapters in which we discuss the requirements of ISO/TS 16949:2002, we've included a section titled "What Auditors Will Look For." Understand that auditors will not be looking for these items in isolation. Instead, they will conduct process audits. These start with the customer's inputs and continue through to the controls for ongoing production.

Another term for process audit might be "multidisciplinary audit." If your organization, from the chief executive to the production workers, understands the significance of this contrast and is prepared for it, your organization will do well.

We welcome comments on this book and questions about its application. You can contact me at *rsmith@patonpress.com*.

—*Radley M.Smith*

Acknowledgments

We wish to thank those members of the Supplier Quality Requirements Task Force and of the International Automotive Oversight Bureau who provided their comments on drafts of this book. We have benefited from these comments but accept responsibility for any remaining errors.

Chapter One

Introduction and Implementation

I f you're a supplier to any one of the Big Three, the large truck manufacturers, a tier-one supplier, or any other automaker, you're undoubtedly familiar with the automakers' supplier quality system requirements. The Big Three, defined in this book as DaimlerChrysler's Chrysler Group, Ford Motor Co., and General Motors Corp., have until recently used QS-9000 as their supplier quality management system requirements. European automakers have until recently used a variety of requirements—including Germany's VDA 6.1, France's EAQF, and Italy's AVSQ—for their production-part suppliers.

The automakers realized that further consolidation was required to facilitate the global automotive supply base and to fully integrate with the newly revised ISO 9001:2000 standard. Therefore, the North American and European automakers collaborated on a global quality management system requirement. The first attempt was ISO/TS 16949:1999, which was based on the 1994 version of ISO 9001. Since the release of ISO 9001:2000, ISO/TS 16949 has been revised and is now officially known as *ISO/TS 16949:2002, Quality management systems— Particular requirements for the application of ISO 9001:2000 for automotive production and relevant service part organizations*. We'll refer to ISO/TS 16949:2002 simply as ISO/TS 16949 throughout this book.

ISO/TS 16949:2002 was jointly developed by International Automotive Task Force (IATF) members, supplier representatives, and other interested parties, such as the Japan Automobile Manufacturers Association. This work was accomplished under the sanction of ISO/TC 176, the technical committee responsible for developing and revising the ISO 9000 family of standards. IATF members include vehicle manufacturers—BMW, DaimlerChrysler, FIAT, Ford, General

Motors, PSA Peugeot-Citroen, Renault SA, and Volkswagen—and their trade associations—Automotive Industry Action Group (AIAG—United States), Associazione Nazionale Fra Industrie Automobilistiche (ANFIA—Italy), Federation des Industries des Equipements pour Vehicules (FIEV—France), Society of Motor Manufacturers and Traders Ltd. (SMMT—United Kingdom), and Verband der Automobilindustrie (VDA—Germany).

Unlike QS-9000, which is not a standard but a body of requirements for production-part suppliers to the Big Three, ISO/TS 16949 is an international technical specification published by the International Organization for Standardization (ISO). After December 15, 2003, QS-9000 became a stand-alone certificate based on ISO 9001:1994. ISO/TS 16949:2002 consists of the ISO 9001:2000 standard in its entirety and additional automotive-specific requirements. Registration to ISO/TS 16949:2002 is sanctioned by the IATF. If an organization wants both ISO/TS 16949:2002 and ISO 9001:2000 on its certificate, it will need to let its registrar know ahead of time. Only IATF-approved registrars are permitted to issue certificates for ISO/TS 16949:2002.

ISO/TS 16949 is more narrowly targeted on the supplier base than QS-9000. The automakers discovered that organizations outside of the automotive supply chain were registering to QS-9000. Although this wouldn't seem to be a problem for the automakers, it diverted auditing and registration resources away from the automotive supply base. Therefore, ISO/TS 16949 only applies to supplier sites that provide automakers with the following value-added manufacturing processes:

■ Production materials

■ Production or service parts

■ Assemblies

■ Heat treating, welding, painting, plating, or other finishing services

In fact, registrars are prohibited from registering organizations outside the automotive supply chain to ISO/TS 16949.

It's important to note that ISO/TS 16949 does not immediately replace QS-9000 or the European automakers' supplier quality requirements. However, all of the participating automakers have set specific deadlines for their suppliers to make the transition. (For example, DaimlerChrysler requires all production-part suppliers to be registered to ISO/TS 16949 no later than July 1, 2004.) In no case is the deadline later than December 14, 2006 (see the list of transition deadlines

REQUIREMENTS AND TRANSITION DEADLINES

North American Automakers

■ *DaimlerChrysler*—Requires registration to ISO/TS 16949:2002 by July 1, 2004.

■ *Ford Motor Co.*—Requires registration to ISO/TS 16949:2002 as optional to QS-9000 by December 14, 2006. Suppliers currently registered to ISO/TS 16949:1999 must upgrade to ISO/TS 16949:2002 by December 15, 2004.

■ *General Motors*—Requires registration to ISO/TS 16949:2002 as optional to QS-9000 by December 14, 2006. Suppliers currently registered to ISO/TS 16949:1999 must upgrade to ISO/TS 16949:2002 by December 15, 2004.

European Automakers

■ *BMW*—Requires compliance only to ISO/TS 16949:2002.

■ *FIAT*—Requires registration now to ISO/TS 16949:2002.

■ *PSA Peugeot Citroen*—Requires registration to ISO/TS 16949:2002 by July 1, 2004. Suppliers currently registered to ISO/TS 16949:1999 must upgrade to ISO/TS 16949:2002 by December 15, 2004.

■ *Renault*— Requires registration to ISO/TS 16949:2002 by July 1, 2004. Suppliers currently registered to ISO/TS 16949:1999 must upgrade to ISO/TS 16949:2002 by December 15, 2004.

■ *Volkswagen*—Requires registration now to ISO/TS 16949:2002 or VDA 6.1.

Japanese Automakers

■ *Nissan*—Requires a quality management system and will accept registration to ISO/TS 16949:2002. Will accept existing other national standard for ANPQP new products.

Nissan is the only Japanese automaker requiring compliance to ISO/TS 16949, probably due to its relationship with Renault.

on page 3). On that date, QS-9000 will officially expire. Suppliers need to upgrade to ISO/TS 16949:2002 prior to the expiration of their current certificate, or before December 15, 2006 (whichever occurs sooner). Check with your registrar to ensure that you meet all applicable transition deadlines. Automotive suppliers need to begin the transition process as soon as possible in order to avoid missing deadlines that may cost them business. The automakers will continue to recognize whichever current requirement is in place until their mandated deadline for transition to ISO/TS 16949:2002.

Because QS-9000 contains ISO 9001:1994, many suppliers have wondered about the status of their ISO 9001:1994 registration. Although all ISO 9001:1994 certificates expired on December 14, 2003, ISO has granted an extension of the ISO 9001:1994 text to be used in conjunction with QS-9000 registration. Again, it's important to note that ISO 9001:1994 certificates are now expired, and QS-9000 certificates will expire on December 14, 2006.

IMPLEMENTATION

Obviously, ISO/TS 16949 is much more narrowly focused than ISO 9001:2000. ISO 9001:2000 was designed to accommodate almost any type or size of manufacturing or service organization; ISO/TS 16949 is focused solely on the automotive supply base. Its function is to identify the required features of a quality management system (QMS) for automotive parts suppliers. However, it's more important that automotive suppliers use ISO/TS 16949 as a reference after they have developed a QMS that adds value to their manufacturing processes.

ISO/TS 16949 is neither a rigid outline for a QMS nor a methodology for developing one. Chapter 3 of this book includes a methodology that has been effective for many suppliers who believe that QS-9000 actually helped improve their company. You might choose to organize your company's QMS according to the six major sections of ISO/TS 16949, but you should avoid using ISO/TS 16949 as an outline at any greater level of detail. That's a sure way to create a system targeted solely at achieving registration. The ultimate absurdity is a procedure written for each of ISO/TS 16949's requirements, resulting in a cumbersome and overwhelming mess.

The automakers' goal in establishing ISO/TS 16949 wasn't to throw more rules and regulations at their supplier base; it was to help suppliers to design, implement, and continuously improve a QMS that provides value to both the sup-

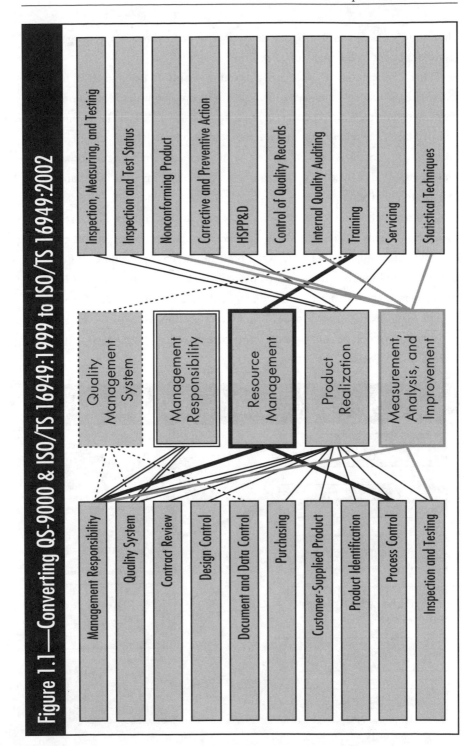

Figure 1.1—Converting QS-9000 & ISO/TS 16949:1999 to ISO/TS 16949:2002

plier and its customers. Your goal isn't to write procedures simply to get registered, but to add value to the organization.

Think of the process as a "gain vs. drain" issue. If the organization views ISO/TS 16949 as a "drain" on resources, it will provide little or no top management involvement, write procedures simply to meet ISO/TS 16949's requirements, and dedicate only one person to write the quality manual and procedures. In this scenario, the organization will end up with numerous and lengthy procedures, view the QMS as a necessary evil, and worry more about getting and maintaining registration than adding value.

Contrast such results with those of an organization that views ISO/TS 16949 as a "gain." This organization will conduct regular top management reviews, employ teams of stakeholders to write procedures, base procedures on existing processes, and improve its processes during the development of the QMS. With this approach, the organization may end up with a minimal number of procedures that may run as few as two pages in length. With this view of the QMS as an opportunity for competitive advantage, the organization should easily attain and maintain ISO/TS 16949 registration.

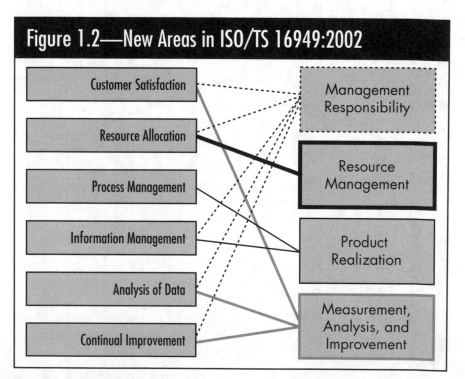

Figure 1.2—New Areas in ISO/TS 16949:2002

Figure 1.3—History

- Mil Std 9858A
- Auto Industry Surveys: Supplier Quality Assurance (SQA), Q101, and SPEAR
- Automotive Industry Quality Programs: Pentastar, Q1, and Targets for Excellence
- ISO 9001:1987, 1994, and 2000
- Quality System Requirements QS-9000:1994, 1996, 1998
- ISO/TS 16949:1999, 2002

In short, implementing and/or updating your QMS to meet the requirements of ISO/TS 16949 should be viewed as an opportunity to add value to the organization. As an automotive supplier, you know that ISO/TS 16949 isn't an optional activity; ISO/TS 16949 registration is required if you wish to continue to sell production parts to automakers beyond the transition deadlines. It's your decision to make the process a gain for your organization rather than a drain. Experience shows that only about 20 percent of suppliers gain added value from their QMSs. Imagine the competitive advantage your organization will gain by using your QMS as a vehicle to drive added value.

USE YOUR QMS TO IMPROVE YOUR ORGANIZATION

"While some organizations have seen the light, changed their cultures, and revised their QMSs to make them effective, useful, and usable, many continue to plod along, not seeing that a continuously improving QMS will make their company more profitable and their individual jobs more satisfying. Unfortunately for them, their competitors may not be so nearsighted.

"The plodders are too busy working to see that, with a little investment of resources and a lot more commitment by management (and everyone else linked to the quality system), the system could be turned into a way to reduce work and improve consistency of operations."

—Roger Frost
ISO Secretariat
Quoted in the INFORMED OUTLOOK, July 2001.

Questions

Where is your organization today on the following questions?

1. Using the implementation approach just discussed, is your company's QMS optimized to the company's needs?

2. Why is your company in this situation?

3. What ideas do you have to improve the situation as your company upgrades to ISO/TS 16949?

    a. Are procedures clear and concise?

    b. Were the procedures written by the people covered by the procedures?

    c. Do the procedures reflect the actual processes?

    d. If the QMS is not optimum, what barriers are there to improving it?

Chapter Two

Lessons Learned From the QS-9000 Process

n 1994, when QS-9000 was about to be released, if a supplier had asked the document's authors how to prepare for QS-9000 registration, they would probably have suggested the following process:

1. Study the new document.
2. Compare it with existing practices.
3. Identify any shortfalls.
4. Fix them.
5. Hire a registrar to confirm that the supplier's practices meet QS-9000's requirements.

For the majority of suppliers, this process didn't happen.

The fact that their customers mandated registration caused what can only be described as terror in the supply base. The involvement of strange-sounding terms like "ISO 9000" and "third-party registrar" made the situation even more threatening. This terror, combined with aggressive marketing by a number of consultants, convinced many suppliers that it was only with outside assistance that they could hope to meet their customers' deadlines. Unfortunately, many suppliers believed that a completely new group of processes, procedures, and activities were required to remain an automotive supplier.

Suppliers often selected consultants (and registrars) based on their experience in achieving client registration on the first try, in the shortest possible time, and at the lowest cost. In retrospect, given this background, the outcome was guaranteed: Suppliers developed quality management systems (QMSs) for the sole purpose of achieving registration. Suppliers wrote numerous and lengthy procedures, which were based only on the consultant's understanding of what was necessary to "pass" a registration audit. These procedures did not necessarily have any relation to the manner in which work was actually performed. Employees were trained to memorize their company's quality policy and—at least on the day of the audit—to work according to their freshly printed job instructions. Just prior to the registration audit, select employees hurriedly conducted an internal audit, and top management set aside five minutes (or less) for a management review.

Not surprisingly, this approach produced the intended results. Almost all suppliers were registered prior to the dates required by their customers. Everyone breathed a sigh of relief and went back to business as normal.

Fast forward to the present and look at the results of this approach. We've heard comments similar to the following quote from at least half a dozen supplier executives: "We've been registered for six years, spent a ton of money, and have nothing to show for it."

Our response is, "Why are you surprised? How much of your own time and attention (top management's) have you given to the development of your company's QMS? How passionate are you about continually improving your company's QMS?" With little investment, there is little return.

In reality, what, if anything, did top management really do to improve the system? W. Edwards Deming preached that the systems and processes that a supplier uses cause at least 85 percent of the problems. Only management can change these systems or processes. Albert Einstein's famous quote on the meaning of insanity applies here: "Doing the same things over and over, but expecting different results." It's up to top management to get personally involved if lasting improvements are to be made to the organization.

It's estimated that about 70 percent of the suppliers that implemented QS-9000 went through the motions out of, if not malicious obedience, at least blind obedience, rather than any belief that this process might improve the productivity and quality of their operations. Although this approach did yield some benefits, they were minor in comparison to the achievements of the 30 percent of suppliers that utilized QS-9000 as a useful tool in the day-to-day management of their businesses. These successful suppliers frequently implemented QS-9000 without external consultants. They simply decided to work to understand the QS-9000 requirements and to integrate them into their company's business.

From the automakers' perspective, the benefits of requiring QS-9000 registration have been less than were hoped for. Although many QS-9000-registered suppliers do an enviable job of meeting customer requirements and shipping on schedule, a significant number do not.

MOVING FROM THE ELEMENT APPROACH TO THE PROCESS APPROACH

ISO 9001:1994, and thus QS-9000, suggests an element-by-element approach to auditing. QS-9000 progressed far beyond ISO 9001:1994 in starting the movement toward systematic thinking, but the inclusion of ISO 9001:1994 limited just how far it could move forward.

ISO/TS 16949:2002 requires a process approach to auditing. This will require organizations to update their thinking in regard to using the quality management principles as outlined in ISO 9000:2000. These include: customer focus, leadership, involvement of people, process approach, system approach to management, continual improvement, factual approach to decision making, and mutually beneficial supplier relationships.

We have presented an overview of all of the relevant documents associated with ISO/TS 16949:2002 in this book. These various documents do not stand alone as items in a checklist mentality (checking off that you have done each shall/item called out in a certain document). They are part of the entire package that automotive suppliers must use to develop a value-adding QMS.

What has been learned from QS-9000 is that organizations can make great strides to improve quality, timing, and profitability if top management understands that a properly developed QMS can help them to accomplish their business objectives. You hire a registrar to audit your organization to the intent of ISO/TS 16949. A registrar's auditor cannot check every single shall; by definition, an audit is a sampling of the process. Auditors will verify that you are following your processes as outlined in ISO/TS 16949. Your organization is responsible, through its internal auditing program and management review process, to verify that all processes are functioning the way they were intended to meet customer requirements. Suppliers that understand the role of the requirements in developing a QMS tailored to their operations are enjoying improved customer satisfaction and continual improvement of their operational metrics.

Chapter Three

Introduction to ISO/TS 16949:2002

This chapter outlines an approach based on the observations of suppliers that consistently provide outstanding quality and whose quality management systems (QMSs) actually add value. These suppliers, if relieved of the requirements for outside audits, would continue the implementation and further development of their QMSs simply because they find the benefits so significant. Some of these suppliers would continue third-party registration even if it were not required, because of its proven record of critically examining key business processes and identifying opportunities for improvement.

To obtain significant benefits from the upgrade to ISO/TS 16949, a different goal than getting registered in the shortest time with the lowest initial cost is required. Otherwise, your company will get registered to ISO/TS 16949 but won't gain anything more than that.

THE ISO/TS 16949 UPGRADE PROCESS

After many years of experience with the registration process and maintenance of that registration, much of the fear associated with meeting your customer's upgrade requirement should have been eliminated. Additionally, the time now available before the customer deadline is adequate for the upgrading of a system that has already been extensively audited.

Considering these facts and the history of QS-9000 registration, the goal for ISO/TS 16949 should be to develop a QMS that promotes continuous improvement of product quality and productivity while also supporting registration.

With this new goal, the development of a QMS will be aligned with the enterprise's financial goals. The QMS will cease being a cost of doing business and become something that actually facilitates the accomplishment of profitability and marketing goals.

Before diving into the upgrade process, the management committee (top management—the chief executive/owner/plant manager and direct reports) must have some idea of the game being played. To facilitate this, we offer a radical but essential suggestion: Members of the management committee must devote one hour to actually reading ISO/TS 16949 and then spend twenty minutes or so writing down their thoughts on how it affects their area of responsibility. (Yes, this means the CFO/controller, the human resources director, the IT champion, and all other senior managers, as well as the one person who has ultimate responsibility for the organization and its success.)

Focusing the management committee on ISO/TS 16949's requirements will help management realize that ISO/TS 16949 is not about paperwork, procedures, and records but is about establishing efficient processes for real world day-to-day business activities and the continuous improvement of them.

THE QMS UPGRADE PROCESS— WORKING SMARTER, NOT HARDER

A group of experts exists who are uniquely qualified to help your company develop a value-adding QMS. Fortunately, you don't need to interview a number of consulting groups or sign a contract to obtain the services of this group. The experts are your employees. They know your company better than outsiders do, and with the proper tools they can develop a QMS that will support your company's registration and be a powerful force for continual improvement.

If your company is currently registered to QS-9000 or ISO/TS 16949:1999, your employees are familiar with the auditing process. The only missing link is familiarity with, and understanding of, the ISO/TS 16949:2002 requirements. This link can be readily provided through training, preferably by your own people who have studied the document at public sessions or in dedicated sessions on your premises.

To use your employees as a resource in developing a value-adding QMS, your organization should follow twelve steps. The remainder of this chapter outlines these steps in detail. As mentioned previously, these steps include the creation of an employee familiarity with, and understanding of, ISO/TS 16949 requirements, at the appropriate time in the process (step 4).`

Figure 3.1—Model of a Process-Based Quality Management System

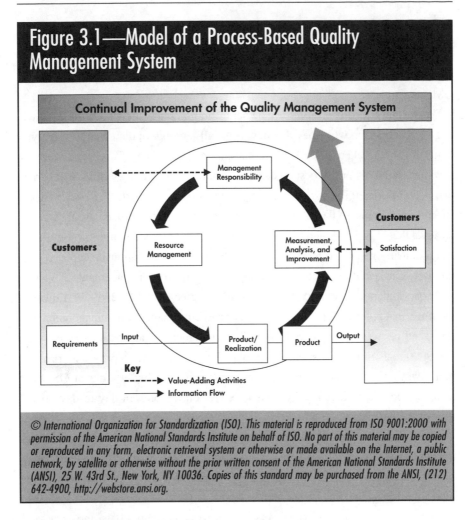

© *International Organization for Standardization (ISO). This material is reproduced from ISO 9001:2000 with permission of the American National Standards Institute on behalf of ISO. No part of this material may be copied or reproduced in any form, electronic retrieval system or otherwise or made available on the Internet, a public network, by satellite or otherwise without the prior written consent of the American National Standards Institute (ANSI), 25 W. 43rd St., New York, NY 10036. Copies of this standard may be purchased from the ANSI, (212) 642-4900, http://webstore.ansi.org.*

Step 1: Provide Management Orientation

Ask any quality practitioner what the most serious obstacle to improving a company's quality system is and at least 98 percent of the time the answer will be, "lack of top management understanding and support."

The issue here is involvement. In the past, it was assumed that a commitment letter signed by the CEO was all that was required of top management. Unfortunately, such "commitment," by itself, has little effect on employees' daily conduct. If the process of upgrading is to contribute any value, top management must be actively involved during the entire process and continually thereafter. This is actually an ISO/TS 16949 requirement, as will be discussed in chapter 5.

It's vitally important that top management understand that they alone are responsible for the system that controls their company's quality and productivity. Clearly, a change in behavior in regard to the organization's approach to the QMS is required.

Most chief executives, company owners, and plant managers have little knowledge of quality, and what they do know is usually wrong. In their minds, quality is either fixed or broken. They believe that quality is a matter of everyone working hard and doing his or her best. If there is a quality problem, they think that someone is doing something wrong, probably out of laziness or perhaps ill will. This is strongly in contrast to the mindset in the typical Japanese company, where a quality level that is good enough for today is definitely not good enough for tomorrow. In this environment, the belief is that employees will continuously improve productivity and quality if given appropriate leadership from management.

Most students of quality would strongly agree with the late W. Edwards Deming, that at least 85 percent of quality problems result from management systems and can only be resolved through management action. However, because QS-9000 registration is perceived as having been ineffective in providing product that always meets customer requirements, management likely looks at QS-9000 as an action taken years ago that has no effect on the present day-to-day operation of the business.

The authors of ISO 9001:2000 understood this perception clearly and, consequently, used the words "Top management shall…" ten times in the management responsibility section of the standard. The intention was to identify the challenges that only top management can meet.

If the upgrade to ISO/TS 16949:2002 is to achieve its goals and is to add value, it's essential that the CEO and his or her direct reports understand their responsibilities and accept them. In the case of large multi-plant suppliers, the plant manager must be a champion for the ISO/TS 16949 process. Although tasks can be delegated, the responsibility for verifying the effective completion of those tasks cannot.

Consider the compelling parallels that can be drawn between quality goals and financial goals. Clearly, companies must return adequate profits to their owners. Elaborate cost analysis and tracking systems are in place to provide the CEO with real-time measurements of financial efficiency. Usually, significant staffs plan these systems and analyze their results. Profitability is everybody's job, but top

Figure 3.2—IATF Focus Clauses

- 4.2.2
- 5.1.1, 5.4.1.1, 5.6.1.1
- 6.2.2.2, 6.2.2.4, 6.3.1, 6.3.2
- 7.1, 7.1.4, 7.2.1.1, 7.3, 7.3.1.1, 7.3.2.3, 7.3.6.3, 7.4.1, 7.4.1.2, 7.4.3.2, 7.5.1.4, 7.5.1.5, 7.5.1.7, 7.5.1.8, 7.5.4.1, 7.6.1, 7.6.3
- 8.1.2, 8.2.1.1, 8.2.2.2, 8.2.3.1, 8.3.4, 8.4.1, 8.5.1.2, 8.5.2.3, 8.5.2.4

management still feels the need to back up everybody with a controller's office or a finance staff.

Just as companies must return adequate profits, so must high-quality products that meet customer needs be provided. This is more than adequately evidenced by the continuing growth in the market share of Asian-based automakers, whose products generally have higher customer-perceived quality than the products of the North American-based producers. However, in spite of this fact, North American-based producers have systematically eliminated their quality staffs. The apparent organizational strategy is that "quality, like profitability, is everybody's job." Training some Six Sigma Black Belts, and letting the employees "fix" quality is thought to be enough. It's difficult to imagine a large automotive supplier in a financial crisis trusting a few Black Belts to turn the organization's financial performance around.

Step 2: Assemble a Team of Stakeholders

Choosing the right people for the ISO/TS 16949 implementation team is crucial. The following criteria should be the basis for selecting team members:

- Familiarity with the company's processes and with top management's objectives
- Familiarity with the current QMS and the third-party auditing process
- Willingness to think outside the box
- Representative of the company's functional departments
- Familiarity with customer expectations
- Credibility with top management

Beyond these criteria, it's important to have various levels of management represented on the team, both to demonstrate commitment and to spread understanding of the process. The size of the team can vary from three to ten, but should be reflective of the size of the business unit seeking ISO/TS 16949 registration. Although team members will generally have other day-to-day responsibilities, it's critical that a significant portion of each team member's time be devoted to the implementation process. The best way to accomplish this is to specify a date for achieving registration that represents a "stretch," normally six to nine months. If a longer period is provided, it's likely that the first months will be wasted.

Step 3: Use Flowcharts to Study Existing QMS Processes

The team's first job is to identify the processes that will be included in the QMS. Without reference to existing procedures, identify the steps in the process and draw a simple flowchart. Although it's possible to use an elaborate system of symbols for flowcharting, it's not necessary. At this point, the goal is simply to show all of the steps in the process and their relationship to each other. A large flip chart or blackboard should be used so that the entire team can see the development of the flowchart, add to it, and correct it.

It's important not to jump to process improvement while developing the flowchart. It may happen that team members make suggestions for simplifying the process before the flowchart is completed. These ideas should be captured and then deferred to step five. Once the team has agreed that the flowchart is an accurate representation of the existing process, the flowchart should be reviewed with all associates involved in the process. Ideally, one of the team members should conduct the review so that comments can be recorded and presented back to the entire team.

Step 4: Identify ISO/TS 16949 Requirements

Training in ISO/TS 16949 requirements should take place after the existing processes have been flowcharted. In this way, team members will understand how the new requirements align with the flowcharted processes. It will become obvious during training that the majority of the ISO/TS 16949:2002 requirements come directly from QS-9000 or ISO/TS 16949:1999, often with no significant change. What is different is the emphasis on processes, rather than on isolated requirements.

Step 5: Simplify Processes While Meeting Requirements

For each process, the team should review the flowchart, keeping in mind relevant ISO/TS 16949 requirements, to see how the process can be improved. In some cases, process steps can be combined or eliminated. Normally, a trial of the proposed new process should be conducted to determine its effectiveness. It will often happen that such a trial produces new insights into the process, which can lead to further efficiencies. Although it's impossible to set any universal criteria for process simplification, the team should be aware that the desired outcome of this process simplification is not the elimination of only one or two steps, but rather 30 to 60 percent of the steps.

Step 6: Capture the Simplified Processes in Concise Procedures

Think of procedures as a tool to communicate your company's best practices to employees. The procedures should be as clear and brief as possible. Forget what your outside auditors say in regard to these procedures. If your team develops clear, brief procedures that cover the "who, what, where, when, and how," they will work just fine. Contrary to what some consultants say, there is no such thing as an "ISO/TS 16949 format" or an "ISO 9001 format" for procedures. Seriously consider making the flowchart part of the procedure (although there is no requirement to do so). Inclusion of a flowchart reduces the number of words required—a huge benefit. There are also major benefits for both internal and external auditing if the flowchart is included. Auditors will understand the process more quickly and determine more accurately if process intent is being met.

One supplier developed a highly effective format that ran the flowchart vertically down the left-hand side of the page while describing each flowchart step in a brief paragraph to the right. Significantly, many of this supplier's procedures were on a single page. Short graphic procedures such as these stand a good chance of actually being posted at the employees' workplaces and used.

Step 7: Implement the New Procedures

The team must consider how the new procedures should be implemented. For minor changes, a verbal review at the job site may be adequate. More significant changes may require classroom training. The rationale for the changes should be explained. For example, "We're making this change to reduce the opportunities for mistakes." Be sure to document whatever training takes place.

If the changes are on a large scale, it may be beneficial to have a limited pilot implementation. If the changes affect more than one location, the pilot could be implemented at a single location only. The results of this pilot can then support the implementation training.

Step 8: Internally Audit for Compliance and Improvement Opportunities

It's common for internal audits to be limited to the determination of compliance. After all, that's the requirement. However, compliance provides only a foundation for continuous improvement. A foundation is necessary, but it doesn't comprise the entire building. For continuous improvement, it's necessary to seek input for process improvements during each internal audit. Suggested questions for attaining this input are provided in chapter 10.

Step 9: Management Review of Findings

Reporting internal audit findings presents the opportunity to obtain management support and commitment of resources for process improvement. Areas such as training, equipment rehabilitation, and concerns about purchased product can be brought forward, and specific requests for resources made.

Step 10: Issue Appropriate Directions

One good way of measuring the effectiveness of a management review meeting is to evaluate what changes occurred as a result of the meeting. What assignments were given? What degree of urgency was communicated? A management review that merely summarizes the number of audits scheduled and completed adds little value to the supplier.

Step 11: Go Back to Step 3

The "Model of a Process-Based QMS" in ISO/TS 16949 makes it clear that continuous improvement requires an ongoing process. Repeating steps one through ten on a regular basis, perhaps two to four times a year, can become the method for a never-ending cycle of quality and productivity improvement.

Step 12: Never Stop

A company that considers productivity and quality improvement of comparable importance to profitability and growth will use the ISO/TS 16949 upgrade process in a way that improves operational efficiency and not only supports registration but also the organization's financial goals.

A company that follows the process described, aside from making solid preparations for the ISO/TS 16949 upgrade audit, will have aligned and integrated its QMS with its business objectives in such a way that the business objectives support the QMS and vice versa.

SUMMARY

This chapter proposes a listing of lessons to learn and thus a suggested process for achieving the ISO/TS 16949 goals. Even if your organization is currently registered to ISO/TS 16949, it would be to your benefit for top management (the management committee) to review what is being done during the normal meetings so as to ensure that the ultimate goal of meeting or exceeding customer satisfaction is a reality for the organization.

It's the authors' firm conviction, based on the observation of a number of successful companies, that this approach will improve a supplier's productivity, product, and service quality, while also enabling registration.

Chapter Four

Quality Management System

S ection 4 of ISO/TS 16949:2002 should be read as an introduction to the entire document. It outlines the basic premise of the requirement: The organization must develop, document, and continually improve a system for controlling and improving the quality of its products and services. For a company that has been registered to QS-9000 or ISO/TS 16949:1999, this is hardly a new idea, but your company should nonetheless take a fresh look at this concept.

Previously, for many companies, the goal was to get registered. We suggest that your company rethink this goal and make it secondary to the goal of establishing a quality management system (QMS) that will help your company improve its quality, customer satisfaction, and productivity. Please understand that improvement in any of these three areas is not in opposition to the others. If your QMS helps prevent operator mistakes or delayed shipments, your organization's quality, customer satisfaction, and productivity will improve.

As you read ISO/TS 16949:2002, use a highlighter to identify each appearance of the word "shall." In every case, "shall" will be followed by a verb that tells you what action is required. But don't think of each "shall" in isolation. Instead, think of the "shalls" as items that you will use to evaluate the completeness of your QMS. Remember, a "shall" indicates a requirement that must be met by your QMS in some way. You and your colleagues have the opportunity to design a QMS that is appropriate for your company while also meeting each of ISO/TS 16949's "shalls."

As you read the document, also note the black lines boxing certain parts of the text. This indicates the text is from ISO 9001:2000. Unboxed text represents the additions by automotive manufacturers. Although there is no difference in the application of the boxed vs. the unboxed requirements, it's helpful to understand which requirements apply to all types of organizations and which apply only to the automotive supply base.

To make finding information about a particular clause easier, each clause begins at the top of the page. In addition, we've highlighted common issues auditors will look for in relation to each of ISO/TS 16949's clauses.

4 QUALITY MANAGEMENT SYSTEM
4.1 GENERAL REQUIREMENTS

The organization must plan, document, establish, and maintain a QMS. The QMS must then be continually improved in its effectiveness. Clause 0.2 recommends that this be accomplished by the use of the process approach to enhance customer satisfaction by meeting customer requirements.

As part of the QMS, the organization must:

1. Recognize the processes that allow the organization to operate
2. Establish the sequence and linkages of the identified processes
3. Determine the effectiveness of the operations and controls needed to run the business
4. Make resources and information available in sufficient quantity and quality to run the business
5. Monitor, measure, and analyze the business to ensure effective operations
6. Take actions to ensure the planned results are attained and continual improvements are being made

The organization must follow all clauses found in ISO/TS 16949:2002 and control all aspects of the business. This includes any outsourcing that might be done, which must be identified in the QMS. When defining a process within the QMS, the organization must describe the management activities, resources, how the process works (usually accomplished by including a flowchart), and how the process is to be measured. Because this is the overall direction of ISO/TS 16949:2002, a lot of issues can be referenced back to this clause if effectiveness of the QMS is found to be questionable.

4 & 4.1

What Auditors Will Look For

■ Evidence that the quality manual and the QMS are in line with ISO/TS 16949

4.1.1 GENERAL REQUIREMENTS—SUPPLEMENTAL

Your organization is responsible for meeting customer requirements, even if some activities in your business are outsourced.

4.1.1

What Auditors Will Look For

■ Evidence that the quality manual covers all outsourced activities and that adequate procedures are in place

■ Records of controls of outsourced activities

4.2 DOCUMENTATION REQUIREMENTS
4.2.1 GENERAL

As part of the organization's QMS, a documentation system must be in place. This system must include a quality policy, quality objectives, a quality manual, documented procedures (see clauses 4.2.3, 4.2.4, 6.2.2.2, 8.2.2, 8.3, and 8.5.3 at a minimum), additional documents as needed to run the business, and records (see clause 4.2.4 for more information). In determining what documents an organization needs to have in its document process, items needed to ensure the effectiveness of the planning, implementation, daily operation, and control of the business must be considered.

Some examples of automotive documentation could include business plans, calibration procedures, control plans, engineering drawings and standards, governmental or industry standards, inspection instructions, job descriptions, job set-up sheets, material specifications, operating procedures, process maps, quality assurance plans, test procedures, or work instructions. Examples of automotive records could include calibration results, contract review results, customer-specified records (such as APQP, PPAP, FMEA, control plans, and MSA studies), design review results, internal audit results and follow-up actions, management review minutes, records of engineering changes and requests for change (both product and process), and test or inspection results.

4.2 & 4.2.1

What Auditors Will Look For
- Evidence of a quality manual and records
- Completeness of the procedures and the QMS to operate the business

4.2.2 QUALITY MANUAL (IATF FOCUS CLAUSE)

This is the first of the IATF focus clauses, which means that there has been a history of past issues in this area and that your registrar will give this clause extra attention. Clause 4.2.2 carries on QS-9000's and ISO/TS 16949:1999's requirement that a quality manual must be developed and maintained by the organization. This document must contain:

- The QMS scope—that is, what the organization does—as well as a listing of anything that the organization wants excluded from the standard (limited to portions of clause 7.3)
- Information relating to any documented procedures that the organization used (Remember that ISO/TS 16949 focuses on customer satisfaction rather than having a large number of documented procedures.)
- A description of how the business operates—that is, the interaction between the various processes (This is a new requirement and includes far more than just flowcharts, process maps, or turtle diagrams. It includes the octopus diagram and customer-oriented process [COP] linkages [see chapter 16].)

4.2.2

What Auditors Will Look For

- Evidence of a conversion matrix from an old quality manual or a manual written to meet ISO/TS 16949:2002's requirements

4.2.3 CONTROL OF DOCUMENTS

An organization establishes a documented procedure in response to ISO/TS 16949:2002 requirements, a governmental regulation, or because the organization believes that it is important to the operating of the business (this includes identified records). When documented procedures are identified, those documents must be controlled.

Clause 4.2.3 requires that a documented process on identifying and controlling the documented procedures in the organization be established. Some of the controls that are needed include:

■ A method to approve documents for the QMS prior to their use

■ A system to continually review and update (including re-approving procedures prior to use)

■ A change recognition process

■ That only current procedures are present at the point of use

■ That personnel can understand the procedures

■ That external documents are identified and controlled

■ That old procedures are prevented from being used

4.2.3

What Auditors Will Look For

■ Evidence that the document control master is up to date and covers the quality manual and the QMS

■ Document approval authority

■ Document approval records

■ Availability and knowledge of documents in the appropriate areas

■ Review and approval of revised documents

■ Storage and disposal of old documented procedures

4.2.3.1 ENGINEERING SPECIFICATIONS

Customer engineering standards and specifications are specifically designated as documents that must be controlled by the organization. These documents must be reviewed in a timely manner (less than two weeks from date of receipt), distributed, and implemented as necessary. A record must be maintained of change dates for each engineering change. This includes the production process changes. A note reminds the organization that all internal documentation (APQP, PPAP, FMEA, and control plans) must also be updated.

4.2.3.1

What Auditors Will Look For

- Evidence that engineering changes have been implemented
- Processes that deal with the notification, distribution, implementation, and control of customer engineering information

4.2.4 CONTROL OF RECORDS

A documented procedure is needed for the control of records within the QMS. This procedure will cover how to determine what records are needed and how to store, protect, retrieve, and dispose of records at the appropriate time. The records must demonstrate that the QMS and all product delivered to customers have met all requirements and that the system is operating effectively—that is, according to the process approach methodology.

4.2.4

What Auditors Will Look For

- Evidence that the maintenance of records is conducted according to both the requirements and the organization's QMS
- Evidence that the record system can be used and maintained according to ISO/TS 16949:2002's intentions
- Evidence that record retention is appropriate

4.2.4.1 RECORDS RETENTION

The organization must meet all customer and regulatory requirements for record retention.

4.2.4.1

What Auditors Will Look For

■ Evidence that records exist and are legible

SUMMARY

The QMS section is a roadmap that the organization must use as a foundation to run its business. With an established management system (which can also include environmental and/or health and safety issues) the organization will be able to focus on customer requirements and working toward customer satisfaction. The organization must ensure that processes are maintained, documented where needed, and that the control of records demonstrates the meeting of requirements.

Chapter Five

Management Responsibility

The lack of significant management involvement in the quality management system (QMS) was clearly understood by the committee that wrote ISO 9001:2000. Although the opening words in the previous version were, "The supplier's management with executive responsibility shall…," real-world experience indicates that "management with executive responsibility" often delegated all aspects of the QMS to the quality manager or to someone with no managerial responsibilities at all. ISO 9001:2000 and ISO/TS 16949:2002 require a supplier's QMS to make a positive contribution to meeting customer requirements and expectations. It's difficult to imagine this contribution occurring without the active participation of top management.

So that there is no doubt about the seriousness of top management involvement, ISO 9001:2000 has nine requirements that begin with the phrase, "Top management shall…" ISO/TS 16949:2002 adds three more. If the content of any of these requirements is not being met, the responsibility is never that of a QMS coordinator or a quality manager but rather that of the person with ultimate responsibility for the supplier (or supplier location)—the plant manager, the chief executive, or the owner. Although top management can and will delegate various tasks relative to the QMS, they can never delegate their responsibility for adequate fulfillment of the requirements of section 5 of ISO/TS 16949:2002.

Your goal should be to establish a robust system that allows top management to measure, monitor, and manage the quality of your company's processes and output. For areas such as absenteeism, direct labor cost, and material costs, any well-managed company will have measurement, monitoring, and management systems in place. The same is required for process and product quality. To develop this system, the starting point is your company's existing management process. Are there regularly scheduled operations reviews? Are key metrics available on your company's information technology system? In short, the QMS should evolve from the way that your company is already managed, as opposed to the imposition of some new set of procedures that are foreign to your organization.

The remainder of this chapter examines the requirements found in section 5 of ISO/TS 16949:2002 and provides examples, insight, and suggestions to aid you in successfully meeting an auditor's expectations.

5.1 MANAGEMENT COMMITMENT

Clause 5.1 defines the overall requirements for top management's involvement in the QMS. It requires top management to be active in the development and implementation of the QMS. This requires top management to be responsible for communication, the quality policy, quality objectives, management reviews, and provision of needed resources.

As you begin working your way through this clause, it's appropriate to start with 5.1's requirements and develop a process for implementing them in your company. As you proceed, you will need to be aware of clauses 5.2 through 5.6, but the last thing you should do is develop procedures for each of these requirements. Instead, develop a system to meet 5.1's requirements and then make sure that the detailed requirements in clauses 5.2 through 5.6 are met by this system.

Fundamentally, clause 5.1 requires top management to develop, manage, and continually improve your company's QMS. If top management doesn't do this, the system will have no basis in reality. It will be a sham, useful only for passing an audit. Clause 5.1 sets out general requirements for top management. These will be detailed in the following sections of this chapter.

Top management must communicate to the entire organization the key constraints that your company operates under: meeting customer, statutory, and regulatory requirements. This requires explaining exactly what those requirements are. Examples include:

- Customer product requirements—dimensional and other engineering requirements, and packaging requirements. Some customers will identify the most critical of these requirements with symbols indicated in their specific requirements.
- Customer service requirements—absolute compliance to delivery schedules
- Statutory (legal) requirements—obeying the laws that apply to your company, such as compliance to labor laws
- Regulatory requirements—meeting the requirements of governmental bodies in areas such as safety and environmental impact

There is a related requirement (in clause 5.5.3) for communication processes to make the organization aware of how well the QMS is actually performing.

Clause 5.1 requires top management to establish a quality policy. This is a general statement that indicates your company's intention to meet customer requirements and states that objectives will be used to measure success in doing so. The quality policy is not the place for flowery language about "being the best" or surpassing all other suppliers. If such statements are made in the quality policy, an auditor can be expected to ask how the company is achieving them.

The requirements concerning the quality policy are intended to counteract the justified scorn and derision this topic received as a result of previous policy requirements. Giving each employee a card with the quality policy, although a possibly useful implementation step, is not the focus of this clause. The entire section begins with the phrase, "Top management shall…"

The first and primary responsibility is to make sure that the quality policy is appropriate to the purpose of the organization. What exactly would an inappropriate quality policy look like? Try this:

Customer satisfaction comes first at ABC Co.

It is our top priority.

We will be the industry leader in customer satisfaction!

Based on that policy, an auditor would expect to see verifiable evidence that management spends more time on measuring, reviewing, and improving customer satisfaction than on any other issue. Further, to verify "industry leadership," comparable customer satisfaction data from all major competitors would be required and would have to demonstrate that ABC has either the highest customer satisfaction in the industry or a plan with demonstrable progress toward this goal.

Although there is (as yet) no cookbook for developing quality policies, there are some guidelines. The policy should:

■ Be concise
■ Be attainable
■ Be verifiable
■ Indicate commitments to meeting all customer requirements
■ Indicate commitments to continuous improvement of the products, service, and the QMS
■ Refer to quality objectives and their significance, but not include them

Once the quality policy is written, it must not only be disseminated throughout the supplier's workforce but must also be monitored, perhaps annually, to make sure that it is still relevant to the supplier. Auditors can be expected not only to verify that the policy meets the requirements but that it also has an effect on everyday business decisions. In short, it must not just "sound good," it must be real.

Because there must be a reference to objectives in the quality policy, the objectives must support the policy. For example, assume the policy includes a commitment to meeting customer requirements. Because one of these requirements is 100 percent on-time delivery performance, it would be inappropriate to have an objective of 95 percent, or for that matter 99 percent, on-time delivery. A match between customer requirements and the supplier's objectives is necessary.

Clause 5.1 also requires top management to establish quality objectives. Top management must be as active in determining quality objectives as they are in determining objectives for sales and costs. There will certainly be staff involvement, but auditors will expect to see evidence of top management overseeing and driving the setting of quality objectives.

Once the objectives are set, if they are to have any meaning, top management, as part of the management review process, must monitor them. An obvious question at this point is, "How can we prove to our auditor that top management is actually monitoring performance to the quality objectives?" The answer is simple: What actions did they take as a result of the monitoring? Because results will often show that the objectives are not being met, management is expected to make assignments as indicated by the performance metrics. If an auditor finds no assignments and no action, this is evidence of inadequate management review.

In many cases, improving quality performance requires resources (e.g., repairing a noncapable machine, training employees, or improving lighting in an assembly area). If specific problems have been identified by the metrics, an auditor will expect to see that management has provided the resources necessary to correct the problem.

5.1

What Auditors Will Look For
- Evidence that top management was active in the development and implementation of the QMS
- Ongoing responsibilities that involve the effectiveness of the system through communication, the quality policy, quality objectives, management reviews, and provision of needed resources

5.1.1 PROCESS EFFICIENCY (IATF FOCUS CLAUSE)

Clause 5.1.1 requires top management to have a method for reviewing all organizational activities that relate to supplying parts to the organization's customers.

All of the requirements mentioned in clause 5.1 are directly from ISO 9001:2000. They apply in all industries and to all organizations registered to this standard. However, in 5.1.1, ISO/TS 16949 adds a requirement that top management must regularly review the efficiency of the product realization and support processes. In simple English, that requires top management to ask how well the core business is being managed. Financial measures obviously come to mind, but from the quality perspective, measures of parts per million (ppm) nonconforming at the customer, first-run capability (the percent of product produced without repair operations), scrap, employee turnover, and delivery performance to schedule are among the appropriate metrics for measuring core business efficiency.

5.1.1

What Auditors Will Look For

■ Evidence of top management review of product realization process efficiency
   ❑ What changes were directed as a result of this review?
   ❑ Is there a reporting process in place?

5.2 CUSTOMER FOCUS

Clause 5.2 requires top management to ensure that processes are in place to monitor customers' wants and needs and to verify that the minimums are being met and, where possible, exceeded. This is a holistic requirement. It doesn't say, or mean, that only engineering requirements define product. Delivery performance, launch support, and on-going support for problem resolution and continuous improvement are also a part of this definition. Customer-specific ISO/TS 16949:2002 requirements are also included. Because all of these topics have requirements elsewhere in ISO/TS 16949, clause 5.2 may appear to be redundant. It isn't. The uniqueness is the inclusion of "top management." If there is any instance of a supplier failing to understand what its customer requires or a failure to meet these requirements, the responsibility is top management's. Auditors will expect to see evidence of the process by which top management meets this responsibility.

5.2

What Auditors Will Look For

■ Evidence of top management's review of determining and meeting customer requirements and enhancing customer satisfaction
❑ What metrics are used?
❑ How is customer satisfaction data obtained?
❑ How are surveys conducted? (Be sure to provide data.)

5.3 QUALITY POLICY

Clause 5.3 is fairly straightforward. As discussed earlier, it requires top management to ensure that the quality policy is suitable, being enforced and improved, supports objectives, and is understood and current for organizational needs.

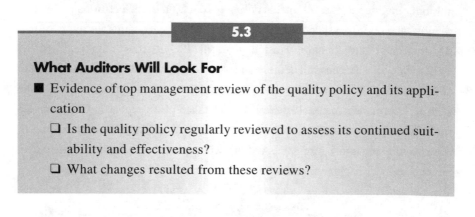

5.3

What Auditors Will Look For

■ Evidence of top management review of the quality policy and its application

❑ Is the quality policy regularly reviewed to assess its continued suitability and effectiveness?

❑ What changes resulted from these reviews?

5.4 PLANNING

The objectives must be measurable and should consider current performance, but always in light of customer requirements. If the current performance is 5,000 ppm nonconforming at the customer, an objective of five ppm nonconforming, although in line with customer requirements, would be beyond the capabilities of most organizations. In many cases, an appropriate one-year objective might be a 90 percent reduction, to 500 ppm.

ISO/TS 16949:2002 adds requirements that top management define the objectives and the metrics used to measure performance against the objectives. In addition, the objectives must be included in the business plan and used by management to deploy the quality policy. In other words, progress against the objectives must be evaluated regularly and appropriate actions implemented, generally in a monthly or quarterly operations meeting (i.e., management review).

The second part of clause 5.4 makes top management responsible for ensuring that the QMS is developed in conformance with the requirements of clause 4.1 and that it is supportive of the fulfillment of the quality objectives. For example, if the quality objectives include a 90 percent reduction in ppm nonconforming at the customer and the quality system provides for an annual management review of customer ppm status, any auditor worth his or her salary will raise a nonconformance that the QMS is not appropriate for meeting the objective.

5.4.1 QUALITY OBJECTIVES

Clause 5.4.1 requires top management to set measurable quality objectives to run the business that correspond to the organization's quality policy.

5.4 & 5.4.1

What Auditors Will Look For

■ The quality objectives
  ❑ How is performance against quality objectives measured and monitored?
  ❑ What actions have been implemented as a result?
  ❑ Are cost indicators and quality indices in place?
  ❑ Are quality objectives linked to the business plan?

5.4.1.1 QUALITY OBJECTIVES—SUPPLEMENTAL (IATF FOCUS CLAUSE)

This clause requires top management to include quality objectives and measurements in the organization's business plan. The objectives should address customer expectations and be achievable within a defined time period.

5.4.1.1

What Auditors Will Look For

■ Evidence that the quality objectives and measurements are included in the business plan

❑ How is performance against these objectives monitored?

❑ What resultant actions have taken place?

❑ Do management review meeting minutes reflect a review of the business plan and quality objectives?

5.4.2 QUALITY MANAGEMENT SYSTEM PLANNING

Top management must make sure that the QMS is planned and maintained. This means that top management is responsible for maintaining the integrity of the QMS. If the position of quality manager were eliminated three months after a supplier is registered to ISO/TS 16949:2002, an auditor will certainly look closely to determine if and how the integrity of the system has been maintained. Without convincing arrangements to assure continuity of the QMS, a nonconformance would be certain. (Unfortunately, the authors' experience finds that this is not a hypothetical scenario.)

5.4.2

What Auditors Will Look For

■ Evidence that top management ensures that the QMS is planned and maintained

❑ What changes have been directed? (Auditors will review internal audit results to see that the QMS is working effectively in a proactive manner.)

5.5 RESPONSIBILITY, AUTHORITY, AND COMMUNICATION

Clause 5.5 contains a number of procedural requirements, which are outlined in clauses 5.5.1 and 5.5.1.1. These support the establishment of a meaningful QMS and cover points that improve its effectiveness. As a foundation for these requirements, top management must communicate the responsibilities and authorities concerning the QMS throughout the organization as a part of the deployment of the system. Operations management must be informed of processes delivering product not meeting requirements. In a stricter evolution of a QS-9000 requirement, quality-responsible personnel must (rather than the previous "should") have the ability and authority to stop production when nonconforming product is being produced. Finally, there must be personnel responsible for quality on all shifts.

5.5

What Auditors Will Look For

■ Evidence that responsibilities and authorities are defined in job descriptions, procedures, and other documents
❑ Is authority/responsibility for quality in the production process defined?
❑ Do those responsible for quality have authority to stop production when quality problems arise?
❑ Are there quality-responsible personnel assigned to all shifts?

5.5.1.1 RESPONSIBILITY FOR QUALITY

Three requirements are listed in this clause:

■ The person(s) who can make corrective action a reality must know when something goes wrong so fixes can be made quickly.

■ People who do the work must be able to stop production if a problem occurs.

■ Any time parts are being made for customers, someone must be capable of checking product quality.

5.5.1.1

What Auditors Will Look For

■ Evidence that all shifts have personnel responsible for quality and that if issues do arise, management is promptly notified

❏ Can evidence be shown that operators have ever stopped production for quality reasons?

5.5.2 MANAGEMENT REPRESENTATIVE

This is the only clause that references the management representative. This person is to be responsible for, and have authority over, overseeing the QMS, reporting on performance, and communicating the customer requirements within the organization.

The requirements for the management representative have been clarified and slightly expanded from those in QS-9000. The first sentence of clause 5.5.2 includes the words, "shall appoint a member of management…" and should be taken seriously. We strongly recommend that the management representative be a direct report to the highest-level person in the organization. Assigning the management representative responsibilities to a quality engineer on the rationale that such person is a member of management because he or she is not an hourly worker trivializes the requirement and by implication the entire QMS. Auditors can be expected to challenge the appointment of a management representative from below the operating committee level. Because the management representative is personally responsible for the operation of the QMS, it's logical that the quality director (or someone from a similar position) be given this role. Furthermore, the ongoing responsibility to report to top management on the operation of the QMS requires an individual with credibility and clout.

5.5.2

What Auditors Will Look For

■ Evidence that the management representative has contact with informed people in the organization (people with an awareness of customer requirements)

❑ Is the management representative actively involved in decisions such as design, sales, manufacturing, and delivery?

5.5.2.1 CUSTOMER REPRESENTATIVE

ISO/TS 16949:2002 significantly modifies ISO 9001:2000 by adding a requirement for a customer representative. Although it's not required by ISO/TS 16949, this should be a person who reports directly to the head of the organization. Although it's possible that the same person could be both the customer representative and the management representative, a better approach is to separate the responsibilities. Logical individuals to select for ensuring that customer requirements are addressed are the directors of sales/marketing and engineering. If the organization has separate teams for each major customer, the head of each customer team might be a good choice for customer representative.

The responsibilities of the customer representative (or each customer-specific customer representative) are listed in clause 5.5.2.1 and are straightforward, but there is one responsibility that needs highlighting. ISO/TS 16949 requires that auditors pay special attention to each customer's specific requirements and that the registration certificate include the names of customers whose unique requirements have been audited. Therefore, the role of the customer representative becomes critical, both during the ISO/TS 16949:2002 upgrade process and during ongoing operations. The role of the customer representative is to be the organization's in-house expert on a particular customer. In addition to being an expert on the customer-specific and purchase order requirements, the customer representative should try to understand the customer to know the customer's unwritten expectations and the prioritization of these expectations. The customer representative should ensure that the customer-specific requirements are understood and implemented by the appropriate people in the supplier's organization. The customer representative must pay particular attention to the selection and management of special characteristics, that is those related to regulatory compliance, vehicle safety, or function.

5.5.2.1

What Auditors Will Look For
- ■ Evidence that the customer representative is actively involved in decisions such as design, sales, manufacturing, and delivery

5.5.3 INTERNAL COMMUNICATION

Clause 5.5.3 requires top management to establish appropriate communication channels about the effectiveness of the QMS throughout the organization.

5.5.3

What Auditors Will Look For

■ Evidence that appropriate communication channels have been established

❑ How do you communicate quality objectives, the quality policy, and other QMS information?

❑ Do employees have ready access to communication methods?

5.6.1 MANAGEMENT REVIEW—GENERAL

Clause 5.6.1 requires top management to be responsible for regularly reviewing the QMS and ensuring that it is functioning as expected. These reviews must include discussions of how to make the system better, and records of these meetings must be kept.

The ISO/TS 16949 requirements for management review begin by stating that they should occur at "planned intervals," yet clause 5.6.1 doesn't define intervals. Your company must determine appropriate intervals based on what is necessary to manage the continuing suitability, adequacy, and effectiveness of the QMS. The size and technical complexity of a supplier's (or plant's) operations will affect the required number of management reviews, but the most appropriate frequencies are monthly and quarterly. A supplier with customer ppms over the customer's target or a supplier faced with a significant number of customer-initiated quality problems should have monthly management review meetings. The input data required in clause 5.6.2 should be provided to management even more frequently, perhaps on a real-time basis.

5.6.1

What Auditors Will Look For

■ Evidence that top management is reviewing all the elements of, and the processes related to, the QMS to ensure its continuing effectiveness

5.6.1.1 QUALITY MANAGEMENT SYSTEM PERFORMANCE (IATF FOCUS CLAUSE)

The QMS reviews must include discussions of performance trends, quality objectives, and the cost of poor quality data. Records must be kept and must demonstrate that the quality objectives are being used in the business plan and with customer satisfaction data.

5.6.1.1

What Auditors Will Look For

■ Evidence that top management is reviewing all the elements of the QMS to ensure its continuing effectiveness

❑ Do management review meeting minutes reflect active management participation?

❑ Are management review meeting minutes retained?

❑ Are action items followed up on?

5.6.2 REVIEW INPUT

The purpose of management review is to give top management an overview of all aspects of QMS performance and to obtain their direction on corrective actions and improvements, as well as to obtain commitment of resources when required. To fulfill this purpose, at minimum, the following list of inputs must be examined and appropriate actions taken and documented:

■ Results of audits

■ Customer feedback

■ Process performance and product conformity

■ Status of preventive and corrective actions

■ Follow-up actions from previous management reviews

■ Changes that could affect the QMS

■ Recommendations for improvement

This list goes well beyond the inputs of many QS-9000 management reviews, which were often limited to a schedule of internal audits planned vs. internal audits completed. Audit results are still an important input because ISO/TS 16949 requires three specific types of audits: QMS, process, and product. However, other data on the operation and effectiveness of the QMS are also necessary, namely performance against quality objectives, customer feedback and other customer satisfaction information, process metrics, product measurement and testing results, cost of poor quality data, and field failure information. These are all the "raw data" for the management review. From these data, management must assign specific tasks, provide necessary resources, follow up on previous assignments, consider any changes to operations (i.e., new product, additional shift, or plant construction projects) that could affect the QMS, and evaluate opportunities for improving the QMS and the need for changes to the quality policy and quality objectives.

5.6.2

What Auditors Will Look For

■ Evidence of management reviews

5.6.2.1 REVIEW INPUT—SUPPLEMENTAL

Additional management review inputs will include external failure data analysis and how quality, safety, and/or the environment may be affected.

5.6.2.1

What Auditors Will Look For

■ Evidence that the additional inputs are included in management reviews

5.6.3 REVIEW OUPUT

There is a clear intent to the management review, and it is in no way connected with meeting a requirement of ISO/TS 16949. Quite simply, the purpose is initiating change in the form of improvement to the product relative to customer requirements and change to the QMS to improve its effectiveness. Obtaining registration and keeping it are beside the point. Management review is how the company learns to improve.

The results of the management review must be documented in a concise and complete form. In many companies, there will already be a process for recording action assignments and tracking progress. If the system is purely electronic, a file copy must be printed out after each management review, as well as whenever updates occur, for review by the auditor.

5.6.3

What Auditors Will Look For

■ Evidence of effective management reviews and their effect on the supplier's processes

SUMMARY

The management responsibility section is a roadmap that supplier management must use to improve their company's quality and productivity. When the requirements for this section are integrated into existing management processes, the resulting processes will enable management to drive progress in quality and productivity improvement. The QMS and the business goals of the organization will not only be aligned, but they will also support each other.

Chapter Six

Resource Management

A s you read section 6 of ISO/TS 16949:2002, look at it as the logical extension of section 5. Section 5 dealt with the responsibilities of top management; section 6 deals with the resources that can only be provided and approved by top management. There is another point in common. Whenever the reasons for an ineffective quality management system (QMS) are discussed, the first factor mentioned is always lack of management involvement, while the second is insufficient resources. Because these two factors are so widely known as causes for ineffective QMSs, the writers of ISO 9001:2000 created sections 5 and 6 to address them.

6.1 PROVISION OF RESOURCES

Clause 6.1 defines the overall requirements that organizations must establish and defines what constitutes the provision of adequate resources to run a business in a way that leads to enhanced customer satisfaction. The organization must function in such a way as to meet customer expectations and other stakeholder needs, as well as part and process performance requirements specified by customers.

One aspect of this requirement is that the QMS is set up and maintained in a way that ensures the continual improvement of the business. Ongoing monitoring of the effectiveness of the QMS, based on the model of a process-based QMS, must show how the organization focuses on what customers want and how satisfied customers are with what they are actually receiving.

6.1

What Auditors Will Look For

■ Evidence that the organization has established and maintained items such as job descriptions, training records, quality plans, shift and supervision staffing, and general and individual personnel workload

6.2 HUMAN RESOURCES
6.2.1 GENERAL

Personnel whose work affects product quality must be competent for their job assignments. The measurement of competency (being well-qualified or capable) can be based on the employee's appropriate education, training, skills, or experience.

6.2 & 6.2.1

What Auditors Will Look For

■ Evidence in training records that personnel have complementing types of education, training, and skills for the job assignments they have

■ Interviews with personnel in jobs that affect product quality

■ Evidence of continual learning in the work assignment area

6.2.2 COMPETENCE, AWARENESS, AND TRAINING

Clause 6.2.2 requires the organization to plan, establish, implement, and maintain records of job requirements needed for the QMS to function. Personnel being capable to do the work assigned to them is important, and the writers of ISO 9001:2000 want organizations to focus on ensuring that personnel are prepared to do the work in an effective manner.

Identifying what an individual is able to do before employing him or her has been the focus of fair-hiring practices for some time. Information about what a job entails is important to organizations so that they can place personnel into positions that they can effectively handle. This doesn't prevent an organization from placing people in jobs that challenge their skills, but proper planning, to ensure the person's success, is required in such situations.

Training can take many forms in today's technological society. Traditional classroom training is still appropriate in many cases, but other forms of training exist as well. These include self-paced learning, audio or video tapes, Internet or distance learning, cable or satellite lectures, and many other media. The learning style of the individual (e.g., visual, auditory, sensory, hands-on) and the person's intrinsic or extrinsic motivation preferences should be taken into account when selecting appropriate learning media.

Much research has been conducted on training evaluation during the last thirty to forty years. One of the best known training evaluation models is the Kirkpatrick model, which consists of four basic levels:

1. Reaction to the training event
2. Knowledge gained during the training event—most commonly measured by pre- and post-test
3. Behavior changes noted on the job by the participants of the training event—usually conducted six months to a year after the learning event
4. Management review of value add in the work force due to training conducted in the past eighteen months

An adaptation of the Kirkpatrick model is the Rice and Munro training evaluation model, which uses the internal auditing requirements of ISO 9001 to collect data for level three and level four analysis. This approach allows an organization to review how individuals are learning and how materials are being used. This method also helps ensure that people are aware of the substance and significance of the work being performed. It can also be used to gather information about how personnel are going about achieving the organization's quality objectives.

Records related to the education, training, skills, and experience of personnel must be maintained. Be cautious in where and how you maintain such records. Check local, state, and government regulations about how personnel information is to be maintained. Generally, in the United States, organizations must protect the privacy of employees; consequently, auditors (internal or external) should not have access to personnel files (personal or medical). This could require the personnel department to maintain a separate file for training records.

6.2.2

What Auditors Will Look For

- Evidence of qualifications for each position and how these qualifications are being met
- Job descriptions
- Training plans and training records that indicate personnel working on product quality are competent for their tasks (This can be partially identified by reviewing the training records and through interviews with personnel and/or supervisors in the work environments.)

6.2.2.1 PRODUCT DESIGN SKILLS

Clause 6.2.2.1 is focused on personnel who have product design responsibility. There is a note in clause 7.3 which specifies that design-and-development planning includes both product and manufacturing process design. Accordingly, in clause 6.2.2.1, product design personnel include both the product engineers and manufacturing process engineers.

Organizations must identify the appropriate tools and techniques to be used by personnel in the design functions. Some of these could include:

- Computer-aided design (CAD) software
- Design for manufacturability (DFM), design for assembly (DFA), or design for disassembly (DFD)
- Design of experiments (DOE)—classical, Taguchi, or Shainin
- Computer-aided engineering (CAE)
- Failure mode and effects analysis (FMEA)—system, design, process, or machinery
- Finite element analysis (FEA)
- Geometric dimensioning and tolerancing (GD&T)
- Quality function deployment (QFD)
- Reliability engineering plans
- Simulation techniques
- Solid modeling
- Value analysis (VA) and value engineering (VE)
- Statistical techniques
- Measurement system analysis (MSA)

6.2.2.1

What Auditors Will Look For

- Evidence of training records that complement the type of design activities present in the organization
- Interviews with design-responsible personnel and/or their supervisors
- Evidence of lists of tools, equipment, software, and other items to be used by product design personnel
- Training records on related items, software, and/or purchase orders of the items needed

6.2.2.2 TRAINING (IATF FOCUS CLAUSE)

This is one of seven clauses in ISO/TS 16949 that require the organization to have a documented procedure. In this case, a documented procedure is needed to identify the training needs and the achievement of employee competence to perform assigned work. The identification of what an employee needs to know is sometimes called a training needs assessment (TNA) and can be conducted either prior to an individual starting a new job or to reevaluate the work that is being done. The focus of the organization in conducting studies of this nature is to review how activities that affect product quality are being handled.

The importance of the need for this information is most commonly noticed during times of rapid change. Common changes that can affect an organization's ability to ensure employee competence may include:

■ Acquisitions, mergers, joint ventures, or other sell-offs of organization functions
■ Assimilation of new technology
■ Introduction of new or major change of product, process, or facilities
■ Rapid growth or decline
■ Rapid changes in the economy
■ Unexpected change in management

The organization should develop a formal method for TNA and for application of an evaluation model to meet the requirements in this clause. At a minimum, a skills matrix will be needed. Special attention must be paid to personnel performing specific assigned tasks (e.g., internal auditors, mentioned in clause 8.2.2.5)

6.2.2.2

What Auditors Will Look For
■ Evidence that procedures are defined in the quality manual and used in actual practice
■ Evidence that training records coincide with the types of special tasks performed in the organization
■ Evidence that training has been provided to satisfy any governmental or customer-specific requirements

6.2.2.3 TRAINING ON THE JOB

Clause 6.2.2.3 requires all employees who affect the quality of products to receive on-the-job training when starting a new position or if their job is modified in any way. This is an all-encompassing statement, including anyone working in the organization, from sweeper to president, who might affect the quality of product being shipped to customers. The organization is responsible for anyone who comes onto its premises to work, including part-time, contract, or agency people who are brought in for short, specific tasks. These people must be included in the organization's training plan.

The second part of clause 6.2.2.3 requires all employees who affect product quality to be informed of the consequences of their work as it relates to product nonconformities. Employees must know how their work affects others and how it relates to the achievement of quality objectives. They should also understand how the products they are making are used. A display of the failure modes associated with each production operation and/or warranty costs attributable to each operation are possible approaches toward meeting these requirements. Working with a local dealership to have a vehicle, or at least pictures of a vehicle, available for employee inspection would also be useful.

6.2.2.3

What Auditors Will Look For

■ Training records for people in new assignments (to compare to job task matrices, or information about new machines, or other process changes)

■ Internal job rotation information compared to training provided

■ Training records for part-time, contract, or other agency personnel who are, or have been, in the building since the last audit

■ Evidence that production employees understand the significance of their specific operation

6.2.2.4 EMPLOYEE MOTIVATION AND EMPOWERMENT (IATF FOCUS CLAUSE)

This clause requires that your QMS has an active employee motivation program which includes three aspects: quality work, continual improvement, and innovation. The quality work should be a result of the quality objectives set forth in the quality manual. All employees must know how their work is important to the quality of the products. All employees should be actively engaged in continually trying to improve their jobs and looking for new innovations that could lead to enhanced customer satisfaction. Consequently, a method for collecting, evaluating, and implementing employee ideas will be important to the organization. The opportunity to investigate new ideas through awareness, understanding, commitment, and implementation should be made available to all employees.

The second half of this requirement is that the organization must have a process in place to measure these conditions. Measures are needed for employee awareness of the quality of their work, the importance of their work, and how their work contributes to the quality objectives of the organization. Besides the traditional survey approach, other methods could include awards, improvement suggestion programs, poster campaigns, competitions, quality circles, training or information meetings, workshops, and/or zero defect programs.

6.2.2.4

What Auditors Will Look For

- Evidence that incentive systems or programs are being used
- The organization's employee motivation program's overall scope and evidence of its implementation
- How the measurements of the overall programs are being conducted within the organization, and how management is reading the data trends

6.3 INFRASTRUCTURE

As it relates to the physical environment that is used to produce the parts, the organization's effort to achieve conformity of product quality must be planned, implemented, and maintained. Items to be considered here include buildings, workspaces, tools, instruments, process equipment (machines and software), environmental controls, and supporting services (transportation, utilities usage, communication, etc.).

6.3

What Auditors Will Look For

■ Evidence that the support structure is appropriately listed in the quality manual

■ Measurement data on failure rates at key points in the infrastructure that point to internal and external product failures

6.3.1 PLANT, FACILITY, AND EQUIPMENT PLANNING (IATF FOCUS CLAUSE)

Clause 6.3.1 adds several factors to clause 6.3. First, in the area of plant, facility, and equipment, plans must be developed using a multidisciplinary group of organization employees. This is to be in line with clause 7.3.1.1's "multidisciplinary approach." Personnel from various parts of the organization must be actively involved with the planning of shop floor usage.

Second, the organization must ensure that the plant layout and resulting work is done in the most effective manner possible. Areas of consideration include optimized material travel, material and product handling, value-adding use of floor space, synchronous material flow patterns, lean manufacturing principles, pull production systems, and the ability of production workers to stop production in the event of nonconformities (clause 5.5.1.1, Responsibility for quality).

Finally, this clause requires that the organization develop and implement a process to evaluate and monitor the overall effectiveness of the existing operations. Some of the factors that could be measured include ergonomics and human factors, cycle times, operator and line balance, storage and buffer inventory levels, inventory turns, use of automation, value-added content, and work plans. Note again that the word "effectiveness" here is based on the model of a process-based QMS, which starts with customer requirements and ends with customer satisfaction. Being effective in what you say you do is not sufficient if the customer is not satisfied with your product. So if you have customers who are asking for changes (e.g., cost give backs, changes in standards, appearance issues of products or packaging, etc.), the organization must find a way to address these wants and needs.

6.3.1

What Auditors Will Look For

- Evidence that teams have and are being used to monitor plant operations and that the teams are cross-functional
- Product results, including internal and external production failures, trends in production, or trends in customer data
- Organizational process flow analysis, as well as current and planned plant layouts

- Metrics that are being collected in the areas of ergonomics, automation, line balance, health and safety issues, government regulation reports, and inventory levels

6.3.2 CONTINGENCY PLANS (IATF FOCUS CLAUSE)

The need for a contingency plan was identified in QS-9000 and is repeated here for events such as utility interruptions, labor shortages, and key equipment failures. The list is not meant to be all-inclusive, so organizations must look at their situation to identify what could go wrong and take action to prevent the interruption of delivery of parts to customers. One item that has been added to this clause is a note on field returns. Field returns can be any product recalled by you or returned to your organization for any reason. A plan of action will be needed in the event a customer contacts your organization with a product quality issue, so that you can contain the problem in-house or replace shipped product as required.

The contingency plan should look at items such as:

■ The availability of alternative remote production capabilities

■ Definition of a responsible person or group to operate emergency procedures

■ Maintenance of a key equipment (machinery or software) list

■ Maintenance operations records

■ A list of personnel contact information

■ Outputs of risk analysis results

■ A process for what to do if a complaint call is received from a customer

6.3.2

What Auditors Will Look For

■ Evidence that a contingency plan exists and that personnel know how to follow the contingency plan

■ Key equipment identification and maintenance records for equipment

6.4 WORK ENVIRONMENT

The organization must plan, implement, and maintain a work environment that will meet the QMS, leading to conformity with customer requirements. This activity should be a proactive and continual review of how products are made. One method to ensure the ongoing suitability of the work environment is to include this in the management review process (5.6.3, Review output).

6.4

What Auditors Will Look For

■ Evidence that the organization has actively planned the work environment according to the quality manual

6.4.1 PERSONNEL SAFETY TO ACHIEVE PRODUCT QUALITY

Some people refer to this as the health and safety focus clause. In this clause the areas to be concerned with are product and personnel safety issues. The most effective way to prevent concerns is during the design-and-development phases of the APQP cycle. Also, during the development of the manufacturing process, safety issues should have a high priority.

The IATF guidance to the ISO/TS 16949:2002 manual lists examples of actions that can be used to prevent safety issues. These include:

■ Defining responsibilities for safety and how to prevent issues
■ Using error-proofing, especially in design and process controls
■ Identifying how to be knowledgeable and current in all applicable regulations (typically done through matrices for the plant)
■ Maintaining safety data sheets where people can easily access the information
■ Reviewing internal/external auditors reports for corrective or preventive actions
■ Reviewing records of accidents
■ Developing a risk analysis of the product (typically done with a system, design, and process FMEA)
■ Using protective equipment, guards, sensors, or other safety-related devices wherever necessary

6.4.1

What Auditors Will Look For

■ Evidence of preventive activities conducted during the design and development of product and manufacturing processes
■ Employee knowledge of governmental regulations and legislation for the appropriate area and industry
■ Risk analysis (e.g., line items in an FMEA) and actions taken to prevent safety and health issues as well as product safety issues
■ Previous internal and external audits results
■ Accident reports in the organization
■ Customer complaints that are safety related

6.4.2 CLEANLINESS OF PREMISES

Clause 6.4.2 requires that the organization maintain a clean and organized environment. The infrastructure needs to be kept in a state of good repair. The organization should be aware of any governmental regulations that might pertain to the cleanliness of the business premises. There may be requirements concerning certain types of chemicals on the premises, which could also lead to health and safety issues. Some customers may also require compliance with, or registration to, ISO 14001.

Cleanliness implementation examples could include items such as:

■ Disposal conditions that are appropriate and meet local requirements

■ Space and storage conditions that meet production needs

■ Machinery, gages, and tools that are clean, intact, and equipped with appropriate safety items

■ Appropriate lighting in all work areas, especially at any inspection points

■ Clear sites for the movement and handling of products (e.g., aisles that are clear for movement, mirrors or other movement aids, warning devices to alert people of moving equipment, etc.)

■ Identification of machinery and other processing systems that are clearly understood by all employees

■ Employee understanding and adherence to cleanliness requirements

6.4.2

What Auditors Will Look For

■ Cleanliness and general housekeeping of the operation in comparison with other plants producing similar products (observed by a tour of the plant and office)

SUMMARY

The resource management section is a roadmap that supplier management must use to improve their company's available resources. With well-trained employees, equipment that works well, a clean environment, and procedures and processes that promote safety, an organization should have an environment that lends itself to the production of materials that meet customer requirements. An organization must ensure that these processes are maintained and working well.

Chapter Seven

Product Realization

What in the world is "product realization"? It's basically an "ISO-speak" word for "core business." Section 7 of ISO/TS 16949:2002 covers the design, process planning, production, and delivery of your organization's products and services to your customers. Because most tier-one suppliers have design responsibility for their products, all of section 7 applies to them. For suppliers that aren't design-responsible (i.e., do not design the actual part that is shipped to the customer), an exclusion can be given for clause 7.3, Design and development planning. However, note that clauses 7.3.3.2, 7.3.6.2, 7.3.6.3, and 7.3.7 will still apply, even for organizations that are not design-responsible.

As you read through section 7, whenever you see the word "shall" ask what your organization already does that meets that requirement. Remember that flowcharting your processes is an invaluable aid in identifying unnecessary process steps, while also indicating opportunities where the requirements of the standard can be—or are already being—met with little or no additional cost.

7.1 PLANNING OF PRODUCT REALIZATION (IATF FOCUS CLAUSE)

Clause 7.1 requires the organization to plan and develop the processes needed for your product realization/core business. The plan must be consistent with the processes and procedures used to establish, document, implement, and maintain the quality management system (QMS). The organization must also:

- Determine quality objectives and product requirements
- Establish processes and documents to ensure that the product meets requirements (This includes the provision of appropriate resources.)
- Implement verification, validation, monitoring, inspection, and test activities necessary to ensure product acceptance
- Maintain records as evidence that product realization processes are sufficient to meet product requirements

Organizations registered to QS-9000 or ISO/TS 16949:1999 will recognize that section 7 of ISO/TS 16949:2002 is similar to the former requirements' clause 4.2.5.1, Advanced quality. Section 7 also includes the same requirements found in QS-9000 or ISO/TS 16949:1999's clauses 4.2 through 4.11, 4.15, and 4.19. Section 7's requirements are second only to those of section 5, Management responsibility, for causing failures/nonconformances during pre-assessments and surveillance audits for organizations seeking registration to ISO/TS 16949:2002.

7.1

What Auditors Will Look For

- Evidence of quality planning and project planning processes
  - ❏ Does your organization use the *Advanced Product Quality Planning* (APQP) manual to accomplish the advanced quality planning process?
  - ❏ Does your organization provide, and have evidence of the provision of, qualified and trained resources for an APQP team to accomplish the advanced quality planning process?
  - ❏ Did the APQP team take into account design/process failure mode and effects analyses (FMEAs) to accomplish the advanced quality planning process?

■ To review the quality plan and design record, control plans, operator instructions, and product approval records

■ Evidence of plans to enhance resources/facilities

■ Evidence of design validation at various stages of the design

❑ Do you have records of design failure mode and effects analysis (DFMEA)?

❑ If your organization has no design responsibility, are there qualified and trained personnel allocated to communicate design information to the organization?

❑ Have your customers reviewed your organization's advanced quality planning process and found it satisfactory?

❑ Are there any customer specifics to be implemented that were missed and/or discovered in the planning and review process?

7.1.1 PLANNING OF PRODUCT REALIZATION— SUPPLEMENTAL

This clause requires the organization to ensure that customer requirements and references to technical specifications are included in the advanced quality planning process and that they are also evident in the organization's quality plan. All customer requirements, as well as the technical, legal, and regulatory requirements, must be identified. For example, are there legal and other environmental requirements that need to be addressed? Does your quality plan clearly identify these issues?

7.1.1

What Auditors Will Look For

■ Evidence of documented customer requirements and technical specifications

■ Evidence that the quality plan includes customer requirements and technical specifications

7.1.2 ACCEPTANCE CRITERIA

This clause is similar to QS-9000's or ISO/TS 16949:1999's clause 4.10.1.1. Organizations are required to use a sampling plan that requires zero defects. Some think that this requires suppliers to deliver products with zero defects. Although the Big Three would certainly welcome a supplier that produces products with zero defects, this is not the requirement. Clause 7.1.2 requires that sampling plans be based on zero defects, which means that the acceptance number for a sample must be zero. A batch cannot be approved if even one defect is found. Multiple sampling plans are not acceptable.

7.1.2

What Auditors Will Look For

- To review the organization's acceptance process and procedure
- To review the product validation test plan with defined acceptance criteria (test specifications)
  - ❏ Has the process or any part of it been approved by the customer?
  - ❏ What is the acceptance level used for attribute data sampling?
  - ❏ In the event of nonconforming product, what is the organization's process for corrective and preventive action?

7.1.3 CONFIDENTIALITY

Although this requirement was in QS-9000 (clause 4.4.11), it was not in ISO/TS 16949:1999. ISO/TS 16949:2002 now requires organizations to have a process for safeguarding and controlling customer-contracted products, projects under development, and any related product information. The process must define the who, what, where, and when, as well as how the information is accessed.

7.1.3

What Auditors Will Look For

■ Evidence of methods to secure access to product development information

❑ How do you ensure the confidentiality of your customer's technical information, products, and products under development?

7.1.4 CHANGE CONTROL (IATF FOCUS CLAUSE)

Clause 7.1.4 addresses the changes that take place in your core business. Historically, product launches are fraught with changes to both design and processes. Customer and organization relationships can be strained by these changes, and they can directly affect the bottom line. Changes that affect product realization are the result of an APQP process that was lacking in effectiveness or of the customer changing its requirements. Many launches of well-received products have been financial disasters due to a poor and/or under-resourced advanced quality planning process. If changes are made after the start of production, profitability can be diminished for the entire model. Management must allocate qualified and properly trained resources to APQP and DFMEA teams to escape changes at this stage from anything other than revised customer requirements.

Many companies have a computer-based engineering change request process (sometimes called an "engineering work order") that links all the areas of the "system" that the change could and/or would affect. This might include areas such as engineering, quality, production, shipping, purchasing, health and safety, as well as environmental, governmental regulations, legal, and other requirements. The database notes the date the change was requested, the organization requesting it, the date change is to be implemented, all areas of the process that are affected, and the approvers of the change. If the change occurs after the initial production part approval process (PPAP), a new PPAP is required. Additionally, design and process FMEAs, process control plans, job instructions, lessons learned, and all other appropriate processes and procedures must note the change.

7.1.4

What Auditors Will Look For

- ■ To review the organization's engineering change request process
- ■ Evidence that changes are recorded and communicated and appropriate documents updated to the new change level
- ■ To follow specific changes through the product realization process to determine if the change control process is being followed
- ■ Evidence that new programs being planned consider changes made in the previous APQP program
  - ❑ Is there a product validation test plan with defined acceptance criteria?

❑ Does the organization conduct impact studies (including proprietary design)?

❑ Does your APQP team have a process to prevent changes?

7.2 CUSTOMER-RELATED PROCESSES
7.2.1 DETERMINATION OF REQUIREMENTS RELATED TO THE PRODUCT

This clause contains the requirements found in QS-9000's clause 4.3.2, Contract review. The requirement was expanded for ISO/TS 16949:2002 to require the organization to identify any known requirements not stated by the customer but necessary for the process.

All of this clause's requirements are deliverables of the APQP team. It's important for the team to identify recycling and environmental impacts, and characteristics that can result from the product and/or the manufacturing process. The organization must also identify federal and state regulations (if any), transportation/shipping requirements of product and receiving, federal and state health and safety requirements, and regulations that affect the manufacturing process in any way.

7.2 & 7.2.1

What Auditors Will Look For
■ To review the APQP planning summary
■ Evidence of statutory and regulatory review and compliance for specific products
■ Evidence of the review of the product's environmental impacts
■ To review the product's recycling processes and procedures

7.2.1.1 CUSTOMER-DESIGNATED SPECIAL CHARACTERISTICS (IATF FOCUS CLAUSE)

Clause 7.2.1.1 requires that the organization demonstrate conformance to customer requirements. This is the same as the requirements found in QS-9000's clause 4.2.3.2.

The APQP team should be able to fulfill this requirement with evidence noted in the FMEAs, control plans, PPAP records, measurement system analysis (MSA) records, coordinate measuring machine check routines, other product-checking fixtures, drawings, and other quality documents.

Remember that ISO/TS 16949:2002 clause 3.1.12 defines special characteristic as a "product characteristic or manufacturing process parameter which can affect safety or compliance with regulations, fit, function, performance, or subsequent processing of product." If your customer does not give you specific symbols to use in designating the levels of control of the special characteristics, a suggested set of symbols is given in the IATF Guidance to ISO/TS 16949:2002, in clause 7.2.1.1.

7.2.1.1

What Auditors Will Look For

■ Evidence of conformance to customer requirements for designation, documentation, and control of special characteristics

■ To review the APQP process for ensuring an orderly communication of the special characteristics from the planning stage through to the operator in the process (found in FMEAs, control plans, work instructions, etc.)

7.2.2 REVIEW OF REQUIREMENTS RELATED TO THE PRODUCT

Clause 7.2.2 requires organizations to review product requirements prior to committing to supplying the product. The review must ensure that your organization can supply the product in a manner that meets customer requirements before your organization commits to making the part. These requirements are the same as in QS-9000's clause 4.3.2, Contract review. This requirement is another APQP process deliverable. The organization has to have documentation showing that it can meet the requirements (via customer specifications, customer approvals, or customer amendments as necessary).

There have been many incidents where companies accepted work only to discover that the tooling required was not compatible with their equipment. The APQP team must determine if there are resources that can deliver the product on time, every time. Many larger organizations have processes and procedures that note the "footprint" of the various manufacturing facilities: equipment size, handling and storage equipment, shipping distance/time/cost, labor agreements, capability data, customer satisfaction data, and the quality and training level of the organization's employees.

7.2.2

What Auditors Will Look For

- The APQP team's feasibility studies
- Process capability data
- Evidence that the review of requirements related to the product was done prior to contract acceptance
- Production volume/capacity data
- Evidence of a defined procedure for accepting new work
- To review product and process changes and the customer sign-off process

7.2.2.1 REVIEW OF REQUIREMENTS RELATED TO THE PRODUCT—SUPPLEMENTAL

Only customers can waive the formal review requirements of clause 7.2.2. This occurs only rarely. Your auditor will require written evidence of this or any other waivers.

7.2.2.1

What Auditors Will Look For

■ Written evidence of customer waivers for any reviews not conducted in accordance with clause 7.2.2

7.2.2.2 ORGANIZATION MANUFACTURING FEASIBILITY

This clause is new for ISO/TS 16949:2002. QS-9000's clause 4.2.3.3 stated that feasibility reviews should be documented. Given all the problems organizations have had with making products according to design, ISO/TS 16949:2002 requires documented feasibility reviews.

This feasibility analysis is an APQP team deliverable that takes place before the design phase. The risk analysis indicates your organization's ability to effectively and efficiently delivers products to customer specifications. The risk analysis should include such items as program timing, required resources, development costs and investments, and preventive maintenance items.

7.2.2.2

What Auditors Will Look For
- To follow several specific products through your feasibility analysis process
- Risk assessments for specific products

7.2.3 CUSTOMER COMMUNICATION
7.2.3.1 CUSTOMER COMMUNICATION—
SUPPLEMENTAL

All too often customers and organizations develop strained relations because of miscommunication or a lack of communication. Customers, organizations, and their support activities are all parts of the manufacturing system that makes a product. Effective communication is required to leverage these resources to provide effective problem solving and corrective action that eliminates problems and reduces variation.

Organizations must develop real-time electronic communication with their customers in the customers' specified language and format. This includes computer-aided design data and electronic data exchange, including product-specification data, shipping information, and all other information that affects the product and/or the customer.

7.2.3 & 7.2.3.1

What Auditors Will Look For

- Evidence that product information was communicated to the customer (This will be required for specific products, selected by the auditor. Examples will be required for each customer mandating ISO/TS 16949:2002.)
- The communication process for order handling
- The process for receiving, analyzing, and utilizing customer feedback

7.3 DESIGN AND DEVELOPMENT
(IATF FOCUS CLAUSE)

Clause 7.3 is intended to cover both the design of product and the design of the manufacturing process. These clauses require something of all organizations. The fact that your organization does not have design control will not free it from responsibility for items relating to the design of your manufacturing and for controls through the life of the product.

7.3.1 DESIGN AND DEVELOPMENT PLANNING
7.3.1.1 MULTIDISCIPLINARY APPROACH
(IATF FOCUS CLAUSE)

The organization must have a defined and documented process for product design and development. An important part of this process is the identification of various phases or sub-processes. Each of these phases is itself a process. Each of these processes must have defined inputs, defined responsibilities of the participants in the process, and defined outputs. There must also be a step that determines if the outputs are an accurate reflection of the inputs and meet your organization's requirements. The successful completion of this step at the end of each phase is often identified as a "milepost" or "gate."

In addition to the responsibilities identified for each phase of the design process, the overall responsibilities for the entire design process must be defined. One of these responsibilities is the monitoring and management of the interfaces between the various phases. A key element in managing these interfaces is providing effective communication between all parties involved in the product-development process as well as with those who develop the manufacturing process that will produce the product. A tool that must be used for managing the overall process is design review (clause 7.3.4), with such reviews held at defined intervals, typically the end of each design phase and perhaps even during some phases.

Beyond these basic ISO 9001:2000 requirements, ISO/TS 16949:2002 requires a multidisciplinary approach to the product and manufacturing process development processes. In many organizations, this requirement may be partially fulfilled by simultaneous engineering. However, the multidisciplinary requirement goes beyond simultaneous engineering by requiring the participation of quality and production personnel in the process. There are three tasks of product/manufacturing process development that must be accomplished by a multidisciplinary team:

- The consideration and determination of special characteristics
- The analysis of potential failure modes and their effects using the FMEA methodology
- The preparation of control plans

Note that the multidisciplinary team is responsible not only for conducting the FMEA but also for taking action the reduce the magnitude of those failure modes with high risk priority numbers (refer to FMEA manual).

Organizations that don't have direct design responsibility must still manage the interfaces between different groups involved in design and development to ensure effective communication and the clear assignment of responsibility.

7.3.1 & 7.3.1.1

What Auditors Will Look For

■ To review the development process for specific products that the auditor selects

■ A review of the organization's product-design-and-development process

■ To review the distinct phases of the design-and-development process
  ❑ What are the exit criteria for each stage?

■ To review management of the interfaces and communications during the design-and-development process

■ Records of the inputs to the design-and-development process for specific products (selected by the auditor)

■ Evidence of changes that occurred to designs and processes due to the FMEAs

■ A review of the control plans

■ Measurements and tests that are the result of FMEA

7.3.2 DESIGN AND DEVELOPMENT INPUTS

The quality of the inputs to design and development can make the difference between a terrible program and a successful one. A record of how your organization developed the design inputs must be maintained. These records must include, at the minimum, functional and performance requirements, appropriate governmental requirements, information related to similar designs, and requirements necessary to your organization's core business. It is strongly suggested that a multidisciplinary team review the inputs for overall adequacy.

7.3.2

What Auditors Will Look For

■ Design-and-development input records

7.3.2.1 PRODUCT DESIGN INPUT

This clause requires the organization to focus on design-and-development inputs and to apply them to the product. Your company must have a process that identifies and documents all customers' requirements, including any special characteristics. Any necessary information that was not provided must be identified and obtained. Any aspect that the customer wanted changed or added during the development process must be noted and implemented. Other requirements to review include product packaging specifications, product identification, and traceability.

A process is required to deploy information from previous design projects/programs, lessons learned, warranty data, competitor analysis, and other relevant sources. Targets for product quality, life, durability, reliability, maintainability, timing, and cost need to be identified and documented.

7.3.2.1

What Auditors Will Look For

■ Records from the development process for specific products that show how the required inputs were utilized

7.3.2.2 MANUFACTURING PROCESS DESIGN INPUT

This is another clause that was not in QS-9000 or ISO/TS 16949:1999. Too often the problems and opportunities of previous programs are never communicated to top management, APQP teams, or to the leadership of new design-and-development teams. Consequently, product launches are often fraught with problems and improvements identified during the life of a previous program.

The development of the manufacturing process must include product design data, targets for productivity, process capability and cost, and customer requirements. Experience from previous developments must be identified, documented, reviewed, and the lessons learned implemented. Error-proofing methods must be developed when these sources of data indicate the need.

7.3.2.2

What Auditors Will Look For

■ To review the productivity, process capability, and cost targets for specific products and evidence that previous programs affected these products
  ❏ What customer requirements have been identified?
  ❏ How did lessons learned from previous developments affect this program?

7.3.2.3 SPECIAL CHARACTERISTICS (IATF FOCUS CLAUSE)

This clause addresses product, process, and test requirements for which reasonably anticipated variation is likely to significantly affect customer satisfaction, as well as safety, regulatory, and environmental compliance. The organization and the APQP team should ensure that special characteristics are identified, reviewed, and evaluated for severity during the DFMEA and process FMEA stages of the product realization process. Lessons learned from previous programs play a key role during severity evaluation. All too often product realization programs are so timing- and cost-focused that top management neglects to apply adequate resources to identify and utilize the proactive/preventive benefits that this process provides. The APQP team must ensure that customer-identified special characteristics of the product-development process and of regulatory and environmental requirements are noted in the control plans, drawings, FMEAs, and operator instructions.

7.3.2.3

What Auditors Will Look For

■ To review the process used to establish special characteristics for specific products

7.3.3 DESIGN AND DEVELOPMENT OUTPUTS

In this step of the product realization process, the organization compares the results of product and process development. For example, whether the design-input records match the design-output records. During the design input process, important information is often discovered. For example, customer inputs are missing or a special characteristic needs to be added. Consequently, the design-and-development output must be in a form that can be verified against the inputs by all parties, including the customer. Any changes made during the design-input stage must be documented in all appropriate records. There must be a documented process for the approval of design outputs prior to their release.

7.3.3

What Auditors Will Look For

■ A process for comparing the design-and-development inputs to the design-and-development output records

■ To review the approval process for design-and-development outputs

■ Evidence of what product acceptance criteria were included in the design-and-development outputs

■ Evidence that product characteristics (essential for the product's safe and proper use) were included in the design-and-development outputs

■ Evidence that purchasing, production, and service were included in the design-and-development process

7.3.3.1 PRODUCT DESIGN OUTPUTS—SUPPLEMENTAL

The design-and-development process has now progressed to the stage where the customers of the process receive their product requirements.

Again, the design-and-development output records must match the design-and-development input records. The DFMEA, reliability results, product special characteristics and specifications, product error-proofing, product definition (drawings and/or math data), the results of design reviews (lessons learned), and applicable diagnostic guidelines must be verified and validated. This requires that all changes made are noted in the design-output documents and in all of the design-input documents. Lessons learned from a specific development program must be identified so that the next program doesn't repeat the same mistakes.

7.3.3.1

What Auditors Will Look For
■ The specified product design outputs for specific products (to verify that the required documentation is complete and reflective of the inputs)

7.3.3.2 MANUFACTURING PROCESS DESIGN OUTPUT

As was the case for the product design process, in the development of the manufacturing process, inputs must match outputs. All documents, including manufacturing process sheets, flowcharts and layouts; PFMEAs; process control plans; work instructions; process approval acceptance criteria; data for quality, reliability, maintainability, and measurability; results of error-proofing; and methods of rapid detection and feedback of product/manufacturing process nonconformities must all agree with the design-input requirements and must all be at the same engineering change level. Lessons learned and customer requirements must match the inputs. Incomplete documentation and traceability in this area frequently lead to problems in production start-up.

7.3.3.2

What Auditors Will Look For

■ Evidence that the manufacturing design outputs accurately reflect the inputs

■ To review changes made during the product design phase (to verify that the process design outputs are all at the same change levels)

■ To review the document control and distribution process for communicating the manufacturing output requirements to the manufacturing organization

7.3.4 DESIGN AND DEVELOPMENT REVIEW

In clause 7.3.1, the organization was required to plan processes to ensure effective communication and the clear assignment of responsibility during the product realization process. Some vehicle development processes note these evaluations as "quality gates" and/or "gate" reviews. These occur at various stages of the vehicle-development process, starting at "alpha" and continuing through to "start of production." These planned multifunctional reviews evaluate each component of the product realization process (inputs and outputs) for their ability to meet both internal and external customer needs and requirements. These reviews must identify obstacles, indicate appropriate corrective actions, and assign responsibility for corrective action, verification, validation, and revision of the appropriate documents.

7.3.4

What Auditors Will Look For

■ To review the design-and-development review process for inclusion of essential features and for effectiveness (based on subsequent production experience)

7.3.4.1 MONITORING

This requirement is new to ISO/TS 16949:2002. The organization is required to measure and analyze the effectiveness of the design-and-development process. The results of this analysis must be included in the management review.

7.3.4.1

What Auditors Will Look For

■ An analysis of the design-and-development process
  ❑ Are design-and-development review measurements, data, and summary reports included in the management review process?

■ To review the risk analysis, costs, and lead-time effects identified by the analysis
■ Evidence of actions taken as result of management review

7.3.5 DESIGN AND DEVELOPMENT VERIFICATION

There is no change in this clause from QS-9000's requirements. The organization must use data to verify that the design planning and development outputs have met the design planning and development inputs (the customer requirements).

Data analysis must demonstrate that the outputs match the inputs, customer requirements are identified, all changes have been documented, and that any actions taken are recorded, with responsibility assigned. The next steps are prototype and pilot.

7.3.5

What Auditors Will Look For

■ To review your company's verification process as it was implemented for specific products, including:

❑ Evidence that all changes for verification and documentation are updated

❑ The process for handling changes identified during the verification process and their effect on timing, manufacturing, and customer requirements

❑ Evidence that the data from the current program are captured in a form that can be communicated to future design-and-development programs

7.3.6 DESIGN AND DEVELOPMENT VALIDATION

Whereas design-and-development verification focused on outputs mirroring inputs, in design-and-development validation, the focus is on ensuring that the product is capable of meeting the specified requirements.

Tooling suppliers conduct capability studies (e.g., circle grid analysis). For example, parts are produced from tooling in the tryout stage and then forwarded to assembly to test welding tools. Tryout parts are most often reworked to reflect the specification requirements. Assembly centers typically conduct twenty-hour runs of tooling and handling equipment to validate sequence of operation and capability. Measurement and other product and process checking systems undergo repeatability and reproducibility evaluation and accuracy tests, with the focus on capability of meeting customer requirements.

7.3.6

What Auditors Will Look For

■ To review the validation process

7.3.6.1 DESIGN AND DEVELOPMENT VALIDATION— SUPPLEMENTAL

The design-and-development process requires the identification and implementation of all customer requirements. Validation must include all customer requirements, including schedules and program timing.

7.3.6.1

What Auditors Will Look For

■ Validation data concerning customer program timing and all other requirements

7.3.6.2 PROTOTYPE PROGRAM

APQP clause 2.5 states that prototype programs are an excellent opportunity for the organization and its customers to evaluate the effectiveness of the design-and-development process. Prototype control plans are required as they are a description of the dimensional measurements, material, and functional tests that will occur during the prototype build.

Prototype parts provide the organization and the customer with an opportunity to evaluate product, process, and service specifications to ensure that special product and process characteristics were included. This allows the establishment of preliminary process parameters and packaging requirements.

7.3.6.2

What Auditors Will Look For

■ To review the organization's prototype process for specific, recently launched products

■ Evidence of lessons learned from the prototype program that can be used to improve the design and the production process

■ To review the prototype control plans

■ Evidence that the prototype process replicates design and production tooling used at start of production

■ Evidence that prototype product is measured and tested to all relevant requirements

  ❑ How does the organization manage outsourced services and subcontracted technical resources?

7.3.6.3 PRODUCT APPROVAL PROCESS (IATF FOCUS CLAUSE)

Although ISO/TS 16949:2002 doesn't mandate use of the *Production Part Approval Process* manual, DaimlerChrysler, Ford, and GM do require its use. As noted in APQP clause 4.4, "the intent of production part approval is to validate that products made from production tools and processes meet engineering requirements." The IATF Guidance to ISO/TS 16949:2002 also requires that organizations use a product and manufacturing process approval procedure with their suppliers.

The organization must comply with every requirement noted in the PPAP manual. Any departures from design requirements must be identified and corrected. If such departures do not affect fit, function, or durability, it's possible that the customer may authorize a deviation from the requirements. In such cases, a signed written deviation authorization, using the customer's established process, must be obtained.

7.3.6.3

What Auditors Will Look For

■ To review the organization's PPAP process for specific, recently launched products
❏ Are warrants properly completed and submitted?
❏ Are documented data available for each of the PPAP requirements for each product?
❏ If there are any nonconformities with customer requirements, has the appropriate authorizing documentation been obtained from the customer?

7.3.7 CONTROL OF DESIGN AND DEVELOPMENT CHANGES

Effectively controlling design-and-development changes lowers costs that affect the bottom line. In one common scenario, customer-initiated changes are made and are not fully documented. The change is effective until those involved in the change process move on to other responsibilities or until variation returns. Another situation is that a change is made to facilitate production but never validated regarding its effect on the rest of the process or on the customer. Most often these changes are dimensional in nature, such as expanding the specification, mean shifting the distribution, or changing the angle of a weld flange. Without proper verification and documentation (including the reason, the initiator, and the date the change request was opened and closed) and an updating of the appropriate documents (D/PFMEAs, control plans, work instructions, measurement systems, drawings, and acceptance criteria), such changes can lead to a whole new round of problem solving and corrective actions. An ineffective change management process is a frequent cause of poor relations between organizations and customers.

The changes must be reviewed, verified, validated (as appropriate), and approved before implementation. Each change must be evaluated for its effect on consistent parts and/or the production system. Remember that changes are permanent in nature and that the people involved in the change process are not. An effective change control process is critical to reducing cost and maintaining positive customer satisfaction.

7.3.7

What Auditors Will Look For

■ To review the organization's change process by tracking the change history of specific products

■ Evidence that records are complete

■ Evidence that changes were reviewed, verified, validated, and approved before implementation

❑ Were D/PFMEAs, control plans, work instructions, flowcharts, process layouts, PPAP documents, measurement systems (CMM specifications), drawings, acceptance criteria, lessons learned, and other appropriate design-and-development records updated to reflect changes?

7.4 PURCHASING
7.4.1 PURCHASING PROCESS (IATF FOCUS CLAUSE)

Stop for a minute to consider the title of this section: "Purchasing Process." As with all other sections, the idea is that there must be established processes for critical business functions that affect product quality. The second paragraph of clause 7.4.1 is crucial: "Suppliers are to be chosen that can provide products that meet your company's and your customers' requirements." It is neither stated nor implied that this is to be the only criterion for supplier selection, but clearly it is a criterion that must be met. If an auditor finds evidence that a problem was caused by purchased product, that's the start of an audit trail that leads directly to your purchasing function. Once suppliers have been chosen, your organization must be able to demonstrate how the purchased products in their facilities conform to specified purchasing requirements.

Your organization is responsible for purchasing products that conform to product requirements. Selected suppliers must be evaluated on their ability to provide conforming products and follow the APQP and PPAP processes as appropriate. An addition to this clause requires organizations to verify the continuity of a supplier's QMS—and its effectiveness—should the supplier come under new ownership.

7.4 & 7.4.1

What Auditors Will Look For

■ To review the process of selecting suppliers and subcontractors for specific products, particularly for any products that have caused in-plant or customer problems

❏ How does the organization ensure that purchased product conforms to specified purchase requirements?

7.4.1.1 REGULATORY CONFORMITY

There is no change in this QMS requirement. Consequently, there is little if any change for QS-9000- or ISO/TS 16949:1999-registered companies. All purchased products and materials must conform to all applicable regulations.

7.4.1.1

What Auditors Will Look For

■ To review the organization's process for communicating applicable regulatory requirements to suppliers and verifying compliance to such requirements

7.4.1.2 SUPPLIER QUALITY MANAGEMENT SYSTEM DEVELOPMENT (IATF FOCUS CLAUSE)

Clause 7.4.1.2 requires that all suppliers be evaluated for conformity with ISO/TS 16949:2002. The first step is registration to ISO 9001:2000. However, some customers do allow various alternatives. An important note in clause 7.4.1.2 adds the concept that supplier development should be prioritized with consideration of the criticality of the purchased product and the supplier's history of quality performance.

7.4.1.2

What Auditors Will Look For

■ To review the supplier-development process for certification to ISO/TS 16949:2002, including prioritization as applicable

■ Copies of suppliers' ISO 9001:2000 certificates

7.4.1.3 CUSTOMER-APPROVED SOURCES

When your customer specifies approved sources of products and materials in the purchase order documents, your company is required to use only these sources. However, your organization is still responsible for ensuring that the products and materials purchased from approved suppliers meet all product requirements.

7.4.1.3

What Auditors Will Look For

■ Evidence that products your customer requires are obtained from approved sources

7.4.2 PURCHASING INFORMATION

Clause 7.4.2 requires that the organization document the product being purchased and the requirements for approval, including procedures, processes, and equipment. Purchase orders and releases are good tools to use for meeting this requirement. Ensure the adequacy of specified purchase requirements before communicating them to potential suppliers. They must understand your organization's QMS requirements.

7.4.2

What Auditors Will Look For

■ Purchase order information for specific products
❏ How does the purchasing organization ensure the adequacy of purchase requirements before approaching the suppliers?
❏ What is the process used to ensure that the supplier has (and understands) all the information necessary to ensure your customer's satisfaction?

7.4.3 VERIFICATION OF PURCHASED PRODUCT
7.4.3.1 INCOMING PRODUCT QUALITY

The organization must have a process and procedures for ensuring that purchased products meet requirements before they are used. Four acceptable methods of accomplishing this are provided, along with the opportunity to use some other method approved by your customer(s). Typically, organizations select from these methods the ones appropriate for particular suppliers and commodities.

Considerations in the selection of these methods are:

■ If statistical data are requested from suppliers, the organization must provide resources for ongoing analysis of these data. Auditors tend to write nonconformities when they find files full of statistical data showing out-of-control and/or nonconforming conditions.

■ Receiving inspection, while appropriate and even necessary in certain situations, generally indicates that suppliers cannot be depended upon to provided quality products. Unless safety, regulatory, or criticality concerns dictate otherwise, an organization should have the goal of developing its suppliers to the level where receiving inspection is not required.

■ The qualification following the third alternative is crucial. Second- or third-party audits are an acceptable approach *only* when supported by documented evidence of acceptable quality. For an organization to claim that its incoming quality program consists of purchasing only from ISO 9001-registered suppliers is to invite a nonconformance.

■ The use of designated laboratory evaluations suggests that the suppliers either don't have the capability to measure their product or that they cannot be trusted. This alternative is generally to be avoided, but is acceptable if there is supporting rationale.

■ Documented customer approval of any other methods must be available at the auditor's request.

7.4.3 & 7.4.3.1

What Auditors Will Look For

■ Incoming quality methods used for specific products that have caused in-plant problems, scrap, rework, or customer concerns

7.4.3.2 SUPPLIER MONITORING (IATF FOCUS CLAUSE)

The organization is responsible for measuring and evaluating its suppliers' ability to deliver product that meets specified requirements, is on schedule, and without returns (product quality and/or shipping damage). The organization is also responsible for monitoring the incidents of premium freight, which is usually an indicator of questionable manufacturing process performance. The organization must ensure that its suppliers are supporting compliance with customer requirements. To provide assurance, your organization must direct your suppliers to gather, analyze, and respond to process performance data.

7.4.3.2

What Auditors Will Look For

■ Subcontractor delivery records on schedule, late deliveries, premium freight, shipping damage, quality-related returns, and other disruptions

■ The organization's supplier manufacturing performance records

■ To review the subcontractor corrective action process and the organization's corrective action verification and validation process

❑ What is the organization doing to promote prevention with the subcontractor?

7.5 PRODUCTION AND SERVICE PROVISION
7.5.1 CONTROL OF PRODUCTION AND SERVICE PROVISION

This clause requires that the production process be recognized as a process and that the necessary inputs be understood, monitored, and managed. The individuals who are part of the process must have the information required to produce the product, including work instructions with an adequate level of detail. The necessary production and measurement equipment must be provided and used. Finally, appropriate production control, delivery systems, and follow-up processes must be in place.

7.5 & 7.5.1

What Auditors Will Look For

■ Evidence that all inputs necessary for the production process are readily available and effectively managed

7.5.1.1 CONTROL PLAN

Process control plans are the operator's "owners manual." They detail for each product and process everything the organization needs to do to ensure compliance with customer requirements.

This clause requires the development of control plans that encompass the entire production system, contain the product and process development outputs, and clearly communicate the key process control characteristics and requirements. The control plans must always be coordinated with the most recent product and process requirements. Some customers require that they review and approve any changes to control plans. As described in the APQP manual, control plans must be developed for the prototype (when applicable), pre-launch, and production phases.

The heart of the control plan is the identification of the specific operations that must be used to conform to requirements. Special characteristics, whether identified by the customer or the organization, must be appropriately indicated. The APQP manual provides the recommended form. The final and most crucial point is that the control plans must include specific response plans when any undesirable measurement results are obtained.

7.5.1.1

What Auditors Will Look For

■ To review the control plans for specific products
   ❏ Do they contain everything the operator needs to know to ensure compliance with customer requirements?

■ Evidence that control plans contain the inputs of DFMEAs and PFMEAs
■ To review control plans to ensure they are at the same change level as the design record
   ❏ Are the control plans controlled documents? What is the process for review and updating them?
   ❏ Does customer satisfaction data provide evidence that the control plans are effective?

7.5.1.2 WORK INSTRUCTIONS

Work instructions are a deliverable of the product and process realization process. They are noted in the appropriate control plan and the organization's quality plan. They are required throughout the entire production and delivery system.

Every operator must have work instructions that are noted in the appropriate control plan and whose content is traceable to the outputs of the product and process realization process.

7.5.1.2

What Auditors Will Look For

■ To review the work instructions for specific products
  - ❑ Are the work instructions controlled?
  - ❑ Are they at the same change level as the engineering records?
  - ❑ Are they traceable to the product realization outputs?
  - ❑ Are they readily available at the workstation?
  - ❑ Does the operator understand them and know how to use them?
  - ❑ Does the customer satisfaction data provide evidence that the work instructions are effective?

7.5.1.3 VERIFICATION OF JOB SET-UPS

Most companies today produce multiple products in their manufacturing systems, so it's critical that they ensure product quality and customer requirements at each job set. A formal verification process for job set-ups is required as the final step and as confirmation of a proper set-up. The set-up instructions identify the necessary tooling (dies, fixtures, molds, gages) and provide process parameter check-off lists and job instructions for all elements of the set-up process.

There must be a process in place with both procedures and adequately trained resources to ensure that all products and processes are verified as meeting the required specifications at each job set-up or changeover.

7.5.1.3

What Auditors Will Look For

■ To review the set-up documents and records for specific products (to verify that they are based on the appropriate inputs and are complete and adequate in providing the information necessary for the set-up)

■ To review the verification process, including interviews with operators and set-up personnel

■ Evidence that the effectiveness of the verification of the job set-up process can be validated by in-plant and customer satisfaction data

7.5.1.4 PREVENTIVE AND PREDICTIVE MAINTENANCE (IATF FOCUS CLAUSE)

The organization must identify process equipment and characteristics whose uncontrolled state and/or availability for production will negatively affect the organization's productivity, performance, quality, and customer satisfaction. Based on this identification, the organization must establish a planned preventive maintenance process. Although not stated as such in ISO/TS 16949, the goal of this program should be the elimination of all unplanned maintenance, such as equipment breakdowns, line stoppages, and any other interruption of production due to equipment repair. Data should be kept to show progress toward this goal and to demonstrate the continual improvement of the effectiveness of the program. Top management must receive a periodic report that details performance of the planned maintenance schedule and shows uptime/downtime information and the number of work stoppages due to equipment problems.

7.5.1.4

What Auditors Will Look For

■ Evidence that the organization has a planned maintenance activity for preventive and predictive maintenance

■ To review the identification of key production equipment and the uptime/downtime records for such equipment

■ To review the effectiveness of the preventive maintenance program as determined by trends in uptime/downtime and production stoppages

7.5.1.5 MANAGEMENT OF PRODUCTION TOOLING (IATF FOCUS CLAUSE)

Your organization must provide competent and adequate resources for design, fabrication, and verification activities. Adequate maintenance facilities and equipment must also be provided. There must be an effective process for protective storage and timely retrieval when the tooling is required for production. An effective process and procedures for set-up (clause 7.5.1.3), for ensuring up-to-date changes (clause 7.3.7), for criteria and schedules for preventive maintenance (clause 7.5.1.4), and for replacement and decommissioning must be in place. Tooling for service requirements must be included in these processes.

7.5.1.5

What Auditors Will Look For

■ To review storage and handling of tooling for specific products

7.5.1.6 PRODUCTION SCHEDULING

The organization must plan production to ensure customer requirements are met, including just-in-time delivery. To support this responsibility, an information and communication system based on customer orders must be in place to provide necessary information to the production activity.

7.5.1.6

What Auditors Will Look For

■ A process for communicating order and delivery information to the customer and the organization

■ Evidence that the communication process is available to the customer

■ To review the nature, root causes, and corrective action for recent shipping complaints

7.5.1.7 FEEDBACK OF INFORMATION FROM SERVICE (IATF FOCUS CLAUSE)

The intent of this clause is to ensure the resources and the method for understanding and communicating how the organization's products contribute to nonconformities external to the organization. Your organization must establish a process for communicating information about external quality concerns to the appropriate individuals within your organization. Data on external quality concerns must be included in the management review.

7.5.1.7

What Auditors Will Look For

■ Evidence of the effectiveness of your organization's programs to communicate applicable nonconformities to the organization

7.5.1.8 SERVICE AGREEMENT WITH CUSTOMER (IATF FOCUS CLAUSE)

This clause requires organizations that have service agreements with their customers to verify the effectiveness of the service centers, tools and measurement equipment, and the training of service personnel.

7.5.1.8

What Auditors Will Look For

■ How the effectiveness of all aspects of the service are verified

7.5.2 VALIDATION OF PROCESSES FOR PRODUCTION AND SERVICE PROVISION
7.5.2.1 VALIDATION OF PROCESSES FOR PRODUCTION AND SERVICE PROVISION— SUPPLEMENTAL

All processes must be validated for production and service provision when the product cannot be confirmed as meeting requirements. The organization must be able to demonstrate that all such processes meet customer requirements. These processes are unique and the validation for each will need to be developed between the organization and the customer. In some cases, generally accepted industry practices will be appropriate, if approved in writing by the customer. The clause lists some possible starting points for developing validation programs, including approval criteria, equipment approval, personnel qualification, and utilization of specific production techniques. The development of the validation process(es) must be documented. Periodic revalidation must be addressed.

7.5.2 & 7.5.2.1

What Auditors Will Look For

■ To review the validation process for specific products

■ Evidence of process parameter monitoring and control

  ❑ Have the requirements for operations, equipment, and personnel been identified?

  ❑ Is periodic revalidation conducted when required by the customer-approved validation process?

  ❑ Are there any customer concerns related to this process? If so, how has the validation process been upgraded to resolve these concerns?

7.5.3 IDENTIFICATION AND TRACEABILITY
7.5.3.1 IDENTIFICATION AND TRACEABILITY— SUPPLEMENTAL

This clause requires the organization to have processes and procedures to ensure that all products (parts, components, etc.) produced by the organization, including purchased products, are identified by their status (meets specifications/rework/work in process) by a means that is readily understood by all employees. All products being produced for shipment to the customer must have a product identifier (tags/bar codes) with part number, the run week/date produced, and, as required by the customer, supporting data that confirms the product meets required specifications. Purchased products and materials are required to have, at a minimum, manufacturing date, product expiration date (as appropriate), product part number/identifier (to ensure first in first out [FIFO], change control, and traceability), chemical ingredients, warnings, and instructions for use.

7.5.3 & 7.5.3.1

What Auditors Will Look For

■ A demonstration of the status identification of any product at the registered site, selected by the auditor

■ How the organization ensures that product shipped to the customer meets specifications, is at the correct change level, is identified, and is shipped in FIFO order

■ Evidence that storage attendants, fork truck drivers, and shipping personnel know product status

■ A demonstration of how the traceability requirement is met (if applicable)

7.5.4 CUSTOMER PROPERTY
7.5.4.1 CUSTOMER-OWNED PRODUCTION TOOLING
(IATF FOCUS CLAUSE)

Clause 7.5.4 contains the same customer property requirements found in QS-9000. All customer property (molds, dies, weld tools, measurement gages and fixtures, internal and external shipping containers, and intellectual property) must be identified. Customer-owned property must have a designated storage location and handling and servicing requirements. Records of all such property must be maintained and communicated to the customer.

The identification noted in clause 7.5.4 must be permanently attached and identifiable on all customer-owned tooling and equipment.

7.5.4 & 7.5.4.1

What Auditors Will Look For
■ Storage and handling processes and procedures for specific customer-owned property
■ Tooling and equipment identification
■ A process for maintaining and storing tooling that is out of current production (service parts)

7.5.5 PRESERVATION OF PRODUCT

The organization is required to have controlled processes and procedures for the handling, storage, packaging, preservation, and delivery of product to ensure conformity to customer requirements. The requirements in clause 7.5.5 are the same as QS-9000's preservation of product requirements.

A key phrase in this clause is "preserve the conformity of product." This includes effective handling of equipment and procedures, storage facilities that protect the product from the elements of the environment, and shipping methods and procedures to ensure the product that arrives at the customer conforms to customer requirements.

7.5.5

What Auditors Will Look For
- To review the organization's product preservation process(es)
- To review storage areas and facilities
- To review shipping and receiving operations
- To review the process to ensure preservation of service parts

7.5.5.1 STORAGE AND INVENTORY

This clause requires the organization to have processes for managing storage and inventory. Aspects of this process must include methods to detect product deterioration, provide stock rotation (FIFO), maximize inventory turns, and ensure that obsolete product is segregated from current production product.

7.5.5.1

What Auditors Will Look For

■ Evidence that the organization conducts audits of storage areas and facilities according to the requirements of this clause

■ Historical data on the organization's inventory turns

7.6 CONTROL OF MONITORING AND MEASURING DEVICES—GENERAL
7.6.1 MEASUREMENT SYSTEM ANALYSIS (IATF FOCUS CLAUSE)

This clause requires the organization to provide effective resources to identify, develop, test, verify, validate, and maintain a system for monitoring and measuring the production system, including product conformance and process capability to customer requirements.

Although the requirements do not specifically reference the *Measurement System Analysis* (MSA) manual, the Big Three customer-specific requirements do. All three companies require their suppliers to use the MSA manual to meet the requirements of clause 7.6.1, unless waived by the customer. The purpose of this clause is to identify common and special cause variation in monitoring and measurement test equipment (MTE) using the analytical methods and acceptance criteria noted in the MSA manual. An often-overlooked fact is that a variation in the measurement system reduces the process capability (Cpk). Therefore, when analyzing a process with marginal capability, it's important to know the variation in the measurement system. If it is substantial, reducing this variation is the first step in improving process capability.

7.6 & 7.6.1

What Auditors Will Look For

- The role of the APQP team in the development and realization process for monitoring and measurement
- The accuracy and precision capability of the monitoring and test equipment
- To review the organization's calibration processes for monitoring and measurement equipment
- Calibration masters and their traceability to the appropriate international and/or national standard
  - ❑ Does the organization maintain calibration results records for all monitoring and measurement equipment?
  - ❑ Are gages studies included in the PPAP files?
  - ❑ Have monitoring and measurement test equipment, and corrective action

and response procedures been identified and implemented?
❑ Is all of the organization's monitoring and test equipment noted in the appropriate control plan?

Statistical studies must be used to analyze variation present in each piece of MTE using the guidelines and acceptance criteria noted in the MSA manual, and every effort must be made to utilize the operators in the studies and tests.

■ Evidence that all MTEs are noted in the appropriate process control plan and PPAP files
■ Gage repeatability and reproducibility (GR&R) studies
❑ Does the organization use statistical methods to check the stability of its MTE on an ongoing basis? If not, then how are the monitoring and measurement results confirmed?

■ To review the MSA conducted for specific products
■ Evidence that regular operators perform the GR&R studies
■ To review the storage, preservation, identification, and traceability of masters

7.6.2 CALIBRATION/VERIFICATION RECORDS

All organizations are required to have a controlled system for documenting the calibration and verification results of each piece of measuring and test equipment used to provide evidence of product conformity requirements, including employee- and customer-owned equipment.

It's not enough to only include part-checking fixtures and gages in the scope. If the organization uses any equipment to make quality decisions, then calibration and verification records are required. Typically this includes micrometers, calipers, torque wrenches, weight scales, and any special purpose equipment for verifying tool-testing instruments for measuring the proper functioning of production equipment.

7.6.2

What Auditors Will Look For

■ A process for calibrating and documenting the results for each piece of measuring and test equipment.

❑ Do the records include equipment identification, acceptance criteria/standard, engineering change level, specifics of stability failures, calibration date, next recalibration date, owner, and department of the MTE as appropriate?

❑ What is the process for identifying and containing product that may be suspect due to measurement system failure? How do you notify the customer? What is the process for release?

7.6.3 LABORATORY REQUIREMENTS (IATF FOCUS CLAUSE)
7.6.3.1 INTERNAL LABORATORY

Organizations that have internal laboratory facilities that perform inspection, test, and calibration services must have a defined scope that clearly communicates the types of work that the facility is capable of performing. Each type of testing that the laboratory performs must be identified in the scope statement. Examples include materials analysis and physical testing, test and measurement instrument calibration, dimensional measurement (via coordinate measuring machines or surface plate techniques), and product testing (environmental, vibration, temperature, or durability). The laboratory scope statement is an integral part of the organization's QMS.

There must be adequate procedures for the work performed and competent personnel to ensure the effective execution of the procedures. If industry (e.g., Society of Automotive Engineers), national (e.g., American Society for Testing and Materials), and/or international (e.g., International Organization for Standardization) test procedures are included in the product requirements, the laboratory must be properly equipped and staffed with personnel competent to perform these tests. One method of obtaining objective verification of the laboratory's competency and compliance with these requirements is accreditation to ISO/IEC 17025. (Such accreditation is not required for laboratories that are part of an organization seeking ISO/TS 16949:2002 registration.)

7.6.3 & 7.6.3.1

What Auditors Will Look For

- Evidence that the laboratory scope is included in the QMS documentation
- How the laboratory scope supports the organization's quality plan
- Competency of the laboratory to do the work specified in its scope
  - Are laboratory personnel appropriately trained?
  - How are qualifications determined?
  - Is the necessary equipment available for all work specified in the scope?

- A demonstration of inspection, testing, and calibrations being performed

7.6.3.2 EXTERNAL LABORATORY

Should the organization contract for the services of a commercial laboratory for inspection, test, or calibration services, the contracted facility must have a defined scope that shows it can adequately do the work. The lab must be approved by the customer (with appropriate documented evidence) or accredited to ISO/IEC 17025 (or national equivalent).

7.6.3.2

What Auditors Will Look For

- Evidence of the commercial laboratory's accreditation to ISO/IEC 17025 and/or evidence of customer approval
- The commercial lab's scope statements

SUMMARY

The product realization (core business) section is a roadmap that the organization must use to attain the capability of meeting customer requirements. Beginning with the receipt of design inputs and continuing through identification of all customer requirements, product and manufacturing process design, purchasing of materials, control of production, and control of monitoring and measurement devices, the organization must take clear and direct steps to ensure product quality and 100 percent conformance to program timing and delivery schedule requirements. Analysis and continual improvement of your company's processes in these areas is vital to both successful registration and customer satisfaction.

Chapter Eight

Measurement, Analysis, and Improvement

Section 8 of ISO/TS 16949:2002 is dedicated to the proposition that your company should be better next month than it is this month, and it should be better next year than it is this year. This is the only viable approach to both job security and the continued existence of your company. However, it's common to hear suppliers claim to already be the best. This could be true, but there are always new, aggressive competitors cropping up.

Imagine this situation: An international affiliate of a major automotive company has built engines for many years in an efficient and flexible plant. However, its designs are old and there are no resources for developing new engines. Then another supplier offers a more advanced engine for the same price, with a transmission free of charge. It's easy to guess what the sourcing decision will be and which plant will shut down.

If your company follows the steps outlined in this book and streamlines its quality management system (QMS) so that it adds value, you will have taken a giant step toward becoming a more efficient producer of higher quality products. However, it is the tools in section 8, along with the dedication of your personnel and the leadership of your management, that will drive your company forward in continuous improvement of quality and productivity.

8.1 GENERAL

Clause 8.1 defines the overall requirements for the organization's measurement, analysis, and improvement efforts. Suppliers must demonstrate that their products meet customer requirements, that the QMS meets requirements, and that the organization is continually working to improve the QMS. There must be evidence that the organization has purposefully planned the system instead of just letting the system evolve. The implementation of the QMS must be monitored through the ongoing internal audit program and through management reviews.

The planning of the QMS must show how the currently utilized methods came to be and how their continued use enhances the operation. Statistical techniques for measuring, analyzing, and monitoring must be taken into consideration.

8.1

What Auditors Will Look For

■ Internal audit reports for at least the past year (one full cycle) and the follow-up actions

■ Product conformance data from various reports (PPAPs, statistical charts, lot inspection records, etc.)

■ The organization's process for monitoring, analyzing, and improving the operation

8.1.1 IDENTIFICATION OF STATISTICAL TOOLS

Clause 8.1.1 requires that statistical methodologies and tools be identified during the planning of new products (APQP). The outputs of this planning must be included in the control plans (prototype, pre-launch, and/or product, as appropriate).

Areas where statistical applications should be considered include:

- *Product development*—tools such as variation analysis, fault tree analysis, regression analysis, correlation studies, dependability analysis and prediction, DOE (classical or Taguchi), and multivariate analysis
- *Purchasing*—product analyzed using statistical methods such as histograms, Pareto analysis, process capability studies, control charts, and sampling techniques
- *Manufacturing*—verification of product characteristics or process parameters using tools such as control charts, histograms, Pareto analysis, variation analysis, and visual graphics to display trends
- *Field analysis or returns*—tools such as dependability assessments, Pareto analysis, Shainin techniques, and fault tree analysis
- *Continual improvement*—variation reduction techniques that use a disciplined approach to reduce waste and improve process throughput
- *Measurement systems analysis*—based on the latest customer-specific requirements

8.1.1

What Auditors Will Look For

- Evidence that basic statistical concepts are present in the control plans (prototype, pre-launch, and production)
- Evidence that statistical concepts were considered in the quality planning documents (APQP, FMEA, PPAP, etc.)
- Evidence that statistical tools are being used in the organization

8.1.2 KNOWLEDGE OF BASIC STATISTICAL CONCEPTS (IATF FOCUS CLAUSE)

Basic statistical concepts must be understood and practiced within the organization. The organization must demonstrate adequate training and evaluation of competence in the use of statistical tools and methods. Some of the basic knowledge required includes an understanding of:

- Variation (part of what W. Edwards Deming called Profound Knowledge)
- The differences between stable and unstable processes
- Process capability (using both short- and long-term calculations)
- The prevention of over adjustment (defined as "making process adjustments that are not statistically appropriate")

Over adjustment (also called tampering) can take many forms. These include setting up machines without reviewing data from previous production runs, operators changing settings at the start of a shift without reviewing data from the previous shift, the settings on machinery being changed because something "does not look right," and management reacting to single points of data instead of reviewing trend data.

8.1.2

What Auditors Will Look For

- Evidence that personnel have taken statistics courses and that their training has been evaluated for competency
- Interviews with various personnel (including managers) to measure how statistical tools and methods are used and understood in the organization

8.2 MONITORING AND MEASUREMENT
8.2.1 CUSTOMER SATISFACTION

The organization must predetermine methods for collecting, using, and monitoring internal and external customer information. For external customers, start by analyzing every point at which the organization has some form of contact with the customer. This contact could occur through design or manufacturing engineers, quality engineers, schedulers, the shipping department, truck drivers, sales personnel, operators, switchboard operators, or any number of others.

Included in clause 8.2.1 is a requirement that the organization monitor customer perception of the organization's meeting of requirements. Customer perception can sometimes become their reality, so an organization needs an early warning system that indicates customer satisfaction with the organization's performance. This perception can have an effect on long-term business opportunities.

8.2 & 8.2.1

What Auditors Will Look For

■ Evidence that customer data is being collected and used to run the business (This includes perception of the fulfillment of customer requirements.)

■ The collection and use of customer satisfaction performance trend indicators

8.2.1.1 CUSTOMER SATISFACTION—SUPPLEMENTAL (IATF FOCUS CLAUSE)

Clause 8.2.1.1 specifies customer indicators that an organization must continually monitor. These can include delivery part quality performance as parts per million (ppm), customer disruptions (including any late shipments or returned parts), delivery schedule performance trends (including the cost of premium freight), part quality issues (both formal and near misses), and any mismatch of part quality indicators that are simultaneously collected by the customer and your organization. The customer indicators that are used should function as baselines for continual improvement initiatives.

The organization must also measure and track the performance of the manufacturing process. This could include such items as first-time-through-manufacturing performance, the number of error-proofing opportunities identified and implemented, the establishment of standardized work processes, lead time reductions, workplace organization, and visual controls deployment.

8.2.1.1

What Auditors Will Look For

- The methodology and collection of customer perception indicators and how the data collected is being used by the organization to continually improve (What are the customer satisfaction performance indicators?)
- A schedule or time sequence for collecting customer information
- Manufacturing processes measurements that meet customer requirements

8.2.2 INTERNAL AUDIT

Clause 8.2.2 requires an internal audit program be implemented on a planned schedule and have the ability to ensure that:

■ The QMS is meeting ISO/TS 16949:2002 and customer-specific requirements
■ The organization is operating according to plans
■ The overall system is effectively implemented and maintained

The internal audit program must:

■ Be a planned event that is actively managed
■ Use previous audits to help guide the auditing sequence
■ Have a defined criteria, scope, frequency, and methods of conduct
■ Employ competent auditors who are objective and impartial in conducting the audit.

A requirement here, as well in ISO 19011:2002 (see chapter 16), is that auditors are not allowed to audit their own work.

Two key factors in this clause are that a documented procedure (one of seven indicated in the standard) must be established, and that records of the audit must be maintained. These are common to both ISO 9001:2000 and ISO/TS 16949:2002.

Management must ensure that nonconformities are dealt with in a timely manner and that follow-up actions, the identification of root causes, and the verification of actions taken be reported in corrective action reports.

8.2.2

What Auditors Will Look For

■ Evidence that the audit schedule covers the entire organization
■ Records of audits that have been performed (These records should indicate what was audited, that the auditors were qualified, and identify any corrective action or preventive action requests that were written. Such records should also demonstrate the impartiality of the auditors, the closure time of findings, and the verification that was conducted.)
  ❑ Was the internal audit conducted to ISO 19011:2002?

8.2.2.1 QUALITY MANAGEMENT SYSTEM AUDIT

This clause requires the organization to ensure that its internal audit process verifies that its QMS is in compliance with ISO/TS 16949:2002 and with any customer requirements. (See chapter 18 for a detailed list of common problems seen in this area.)

8.2.2.1

What Auditors Will Look For

■ Evidence that an audit plan and schedule covers the entire organization's QMS

■ Evidence that the current QMS process is affected by the results of past internal audits

8.2.2.2 MANUFACTURING PROCESS AUDIT (IATF FOCUS CLAUSE)

The internal audit program must review all aspects of the manufacturing process within the organization. This audit must focus on the effectiveness of the processes.

8.2.2.2

What Auditors Will Look For

- To review customer performance indicators that are being collected by the organization
- The corrective action and preventive action requests being written by the internal audit program

8.2.2.3 PRODUCT AUDIT

Production and products must be audited/inspected at designated stages of the manufacturing process at a defined interval to ensure conformance to customer requirements. Such inspection can include focus on items such as product dimensions, appearance, functionality, packaging, labeling, and material content.

8.2.2.3

What Auditors Will Look For

■ Production records indicating the inspection and audit results

8.2.2.4 INTERNAL AUDIT PLANS

An annual plan must exist to ensure that the entire organization's manufacturing-related process is audited and that all production shifts are checked. If nonconformities are found, the audit frequency of that area needs to be adjusted accordingly. A note in the clause indicates that internal auditors should use checklists.

The annual audit plan should be based on factors such as:

- Adequacy and accuracy of performance indicators
- Cost of poor quality data
- The use of statistical techniques
- Capability results
- How an area or department is operating
- Areas that have opportunities for improvement
- Measurement results
- Customer perception indicators
- Supplier performance indicators or other data that could indicate issues or opportunities for continual improvement

---

8.2.2.4

What Auditors Will Look For

- The organization's review of information to set the audit plan and the actual schedule of internal audits
- Indications that an appropriate prioritization is being used in the internal audit process

8.2.2.5 INTERNAL AUDITOR QUALIFICATION

The organization must ensure that qualified auditors are being used in the internal audit program. The qualifications should be defined by customer-specific requirements.

8.2.2.5

What Auditors Will Look For

■ Compliance to customer requirements and ISO 19011:2002

■ Evidence that the organization's procedures are aligned with clause 6.2.2.2

8.2.3 MONITORING AND MEASUREMENT OF PROCESSES

The QMS must be monitored and measured at points in the process that allow for assurance that planned results are being achieved. This is sometimes done by placing dashboards or balanced scorecards at the end of production lines. However your organization establishes the process, corrective action must be taken when planned results are not being met. The choice of measures must be appropriate for the situation and may require careful study to identify the most logical methods to employ.

8.2.3

What Auditors Will Look For

- Evidence of methods used to monitor and measure the QMS processes
- Results of the monitoring and measurement processes (If trends are not according to what was planned, then what corrective action has been taken?)

8.2.3.1 MONITORING AND MEASUREMENT OF MANUFACTURING PROCESSES (IATF FOCUS CLAUSE)

This automotive clause is typically cited to support use of the automotive core tool manuals to assist in monitoring the manufacturing process. Studies must be done on all new products to ensure the capability of the organization to meet customer requirements. The results of these studies must be documented and should include a flow of information from APQP to FMEA, to PPAP, to control plans, to operator instructions. Process objectives such as manufacturing process capability, reliability, maintainability, and availability must be established and acceptance criteria maintained.

The organization must maintain manufacturing process capability and performance, based on the signed-off customer part-approval process. Control plans and process flow diagrams must be followed. This includes maintaining measurement techniques, sampling plans, acceptance criteria, and reaction plans. Monitoring the process over time (trend analysis) should be done to evaluate stability and capability to customer requirements, and to help determine levels of continual improvement efforts.

The organization must maintain records of major changes to the manufacturing process. These records should include items such as material changeover, tooling changes or repairs, machine repairs, and preventive maintenance performed. The records must show the dates of the process changes.

If anything deviates from the planned results, the organization must initiate a reaction plan to address the issue. The formal corrective action process that the organization should follow must include containment actions for suspect product, 100-percent inspection (if appropriate), specific timing to complete activities, assignment of responsibility, and customer approval (when necessary).

8.2.3.1

What Auditors Will Look For

- Preliminary process capability results and production control plans
- Process studies using actual production tooling or surrogate production to simulate new part production characteristics
- Documents relating to the monitoring and measurement of manufacturing processes

- Cpk and Ppk data in line with customer requirements
- Review of current production methods in line with control plans and process maps
- Review of APQP, FMEA, PPAP, and other related documents in comparison with the current manufacturing processes
- Review of control charts being used in the manufacturing process
- Corrective action reports and verification of actions taken
- Records of manufacturing process changes

8.2.4 MONITORING AND MEASUREMENT OF PRODUCT

The product characteristics must be monitored and measured to ensure that all customer requirements and organizational goals are being met. These studies are to be conducted at planned intervals during the manufacturing process. Records of conformity must be maintained and should contain information relating to the types of measurement performed, the conditions under which the tests were run, and the capability and skills of the test operators. Product, for either customer production or service, is only to be released by the organization when all requirements are met, unless otherwise directed by the customer.

8.2.4

What Auditors Will Look For

- Inspection instructions and evidence that control plans are being followed
- Records of completed tests
- Inspection records that indicate acceptance criteria, operator qualifications, and conditions under which the tests were completed

8.2.4.1 LAYOUT INSPECTION AND FUNCTIONAL TESTING

Layout inspection should be conducted in accordance with the control plans and must be in line with customer requirements (see DaimlerChrysler and Ford customer-specific requirements for yearly layouts). The layout inspection is defined as a complete measurement of all product dimensions as they are shown in the design records. Results of all layout inspections are to be made available for customer review if requested.

8.2.4.1

What Auditors Will Look For

■ Evidence that layouts have been completed in a timely manner and according to the control plans

■ Records indicating that all items meet customer requirements or that appropriate corrective action was taken when customer requirements were not met

8.2.4.2 APPEARANCE ITEMS

Appearance characteristics must be closely monitored due to the inherent subjectivity of most tests. Appropriate environmental issues, such as adequate lighting for evaluation, masters (including color, grains, gloss, metallic brilliance, etc.), maintenance and control of the masters (to ensure that they remain in specification), and assurance of continuing maintenance of employee competence to conduct these tests, must be maintained.

8.2.4.2

What Auditors Will Look For

■ Evidence that training records of test operators, visual aids, masters, and other appearance-checking instruments are maintained

8.3 CONTROL OF NONCONFORMING PRODUCT

If product or material is found to be nonconforming, then action must be taken to prevent the use or shipment of that product. The organization must have a documented procedure to communicate responsibilities for handling nonconformities.

The organization must deal with nonconforming product in one of three ways:

■ Detect and eliminate the root cause of the situation

■ Authorize, through customer or other authority concession, the use of the product as is, or a rework of the product

■ Modify the nonconforming product in such a way as to prevent its use

The organization must maintain records of any nonconforming product issues and the actions that were taken. If product is reworked, then re-verification is needed to ensure conformity to all requirements. If nonconforming product is detected after shipment to a customer, then proactive action must be taken to diminish adverse effects to the customer.

8.3

What Auditors Will Look For

■ Evidence that that a documented procedure is in use for nonconforming products

■ Records of how nonconforming product has been dealt with

8.3.1 CONTROL OF NONCONFORMING PRODUCT—SUPPLEMENTAL

Product or materials that cannot be positively identified as meeting customer requirements must be considered nonconforming product until proven otherwise.

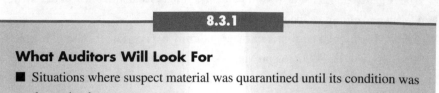

What Auditors Will Look For

■ Situations where suspect material was quarantined until its condition was determined

8.3.2 CONTROL OF REWORKED PRODUCT

Rework instructions must be available to the personnel involved in the rework process. This must include instructions for re-inspecting the product.

8.3.2

What Auditors Will Look For

■ Evidence of rework instructions at the appropriate locations

8.3.3 CUSTOMER INFORMATION

Clause 8.3.3 requires the organization to warn customers if nonconforming product has been inadvertently shipped.

8.3.3

What Auditors Will Look For

■ Records that might indicate that this requirement was needed and what was done to meet the requirement

8.3.4 CUSTOMER WAIVER (IATF FOCUS CLAUSE)

If nonconforming product is detected in the organization's process, the process must be stopped until a customer concession or deviation permit is obtained or other required action completed. In these situations, the organization must maintain records of expiration dates, quantities authorized, when the process returned to normal production, and material identification of any materials shipped under waiver. This must reach back into the organization's supplier channels to ensure that all products meet requirements. The organization is responsible to ensure that all product shipped to customers meets requirements.

8.3.4

What Auditors Will Look For

■ Evidence that the organization can meet requirements as set forth in ISO/TS 16949:2002 and in accordance with the QMS

8.4 ANALYSIS OF DATA

The practice of planning, collecting, and studying data must be established by the organization and must lead to a demonstration that the QMS is both suitable and effective. Internal performance data could include items such as cost of poor quality, efficiency of production processes, test results, process capability information, quality audits, internal audits, employee suggestion programs, and customer reports.

The collection of this information must lead to the identification and implementation of continual improvement in the QMS. Information that must be studied includes customer satisfaction, product conformity, data trends, opportunities for preventive action, and supplier data.

8.4

What Auditors Will Look For

■ Trends in the internal and external performance metrics

8.4.1 ANALYSIS AND USE OF DATA (IATF FOCUS CLAUSE)

The organization must review the trends in quality and operational performance metrics to ensure that the business objectives are being met. These objectives must include a process that quickly resolves any customer-related problems, identifies key customer-related trends, and takes actions to meet future needs, as well as an information system that quickly reports to the organization any product usage issues. Comparison data should be sought on competitors and/or other appropriate benchmarks.

8.4.1

What Auditors Will Look For

- Comparison information between trend data and organizational goals and objectives
- Indications that the organization is taking appropriate actions when needed

8.5 IMPROVEMENT
8.5.1 CONTINUAL IMPROVEMENT

The organization must strive to continually improve the effectiveness of its QMS by using the quality policy, quality objectives, internal audit results, the analysis of data, both corrective and preventive actions, and the management review activities.

8.5 & 8.5.1

What Auditors Will Look For

■ Evidence that the named processes are being used to continually improve the QMS

8.5.1.1 CONTINUAL IMPROVEMENT OF THE ORGANIZATION

The organization is directed to define a process for continual improvement using Annex B of ISO 9004:2000. The continual improvement method should include the following:

■ The reason for the improvement

■ The current condition

■ Root cause identification

■ Identification of possible solutions

■ Evaluation of the effects of those solutions

■ Use of the plan-do-study-act cycle (PDSA) with the new process

■ Comparison to the benchmark and confirmation of effectiveness and efficiency

There are two basic ways to conduct continual process improvements: through small step-by-step improvement activities, or through breakthrough projects. Some of the formal programs that assist in these efforts are the Six Sigma or Shainin Red X methodologies. In either case, your organization will need to use some form of W. Edwards Deming's plan-do-study-act model to make improvements to the QMS.

Breakthrough projects usually involve a significant redesign of existing processes and the organization must be ready to support these major efforts. The overall process for improvement should be repeated continually. Everyone in the organization must be aware of and support the improvement initiatives. Some tools that can be used on their own or in conjunction with major improvement methodologies are capability studies, cause-and-effect diagrams, design of experiments, run charts, control charts, risk analysis, supplier evaluations, flowcharts, histograms, Pareto charts, theory of constraints, ppm studies, value analysis, value engineering, benchmarking, and error-proofing or other variation reduction tools.

8.5.1.1

What Auditors Will Look For

■ Evidence of a procedure in the quality manual and active use of the methodology chosen by the organization

8.5.1.2 MANUFACTURING PROCESS IMPROVEMENT (IATF FOCUS CLAUSE)

The manufacturing processes in the organization must first be capable and in a state of stability. Then the organization, using the control plan as a primary document, must continually focus on controls and reducing variation in process parameters and product characteristics.

8.5.1.2

What Auditors Will Look For

■ Records of variation reduction projects and their results

8.5.2 CORRECTIVE ACTION

Similar to QS-9000, clause 8.5.2 is another area where a documented procedure is required. Most organizations already have a documented procedure that outlines the steps to eliminate the causes of nonconformities that have been found in a process. The focus must be a system that prevents the recurrence of identified nonconformities by reviewing nonconformities that have occurred, reviewing customer complaints, determining the root causes of the issues, evaluating the actions needed to prevent future issues, implementing a solution, recording the results, and reviewing the actions taken to ensure issues do not return.

8.5.2

What Auditors Will Look For

- Evidence that successful corrective action projects have occurred and have been effective
- Evidence that customer complaints have been addressed using the corrective action process

8.5.2.1 PROBLEM SOLVING

The organization must have a defined process for solving problems. This process is to focus on root cause analysis and elimination. Most problem-solving approaches have at least four steps:

1. Problem identification
2. Containment
3. Root cause identification
4. Verification of effectiveness of corrective action

Many customers will have a preferred problem-solving process, and if required, the organization must use what its customer requests. Some of the more well-known processes are: Kepner-Tregoe, DaimlerChrysler Seven Step, Ford Global Eight Disciplines, and GM Problem Reporting and Resolution.

Some common tools that have been found useful in problem-solving efforts include failure mode analysis, capability studies, regression/correlation studies, cause-and-effect diagrams, FMEAs, histograms, run charts, Pareto analysis, probability studies, use of graphical techniques, and stratification studies.

8.5.2.1

What Auditors Will Look For

■ Evidence that responses have been given to customer complaints, using the customer's formats

■ Evidence that a problem-solving process is in place and is being used effectively

8.5.2.2 ERROR-PROOFING

The corrective action process must use error-proofing to prevent recurrence. Other names for this technique include *poka-yoke* or mistake-proofing.

8.5.2.2

What Auditors Will Look For

■ Evidence of successful examples of error-proofing application

8.5.2.3 CORRECTIVE ACTION IMPACT
(IATF FOCUS CLAUSE)

Once corrective actions have proven successful in preventing recurrence, the organization must seek similar situations where the technique can be utilized to prevent issues in other areas.

8.5.2.3

What Auditors Will Look For

■ Evidence that lessons learned from corrective action have been applied to other areas

8.5.2.4 REJECTED PRODUCT TEST/ANALYSIS (IATF FOCUS CLAUSE)

The organization must study all external failures and look for ways to prevent future issues. The cycle time of these studies must be reduced and records of the studies and results kept for review by customers, if requested. Some tools that can be used in these studies include failure mode analysis, capability studies, correlation studies, cause-and-effect diagrams, FMEAs, histograms, Pareto studies, probability charts, and other problem-solving methodologies.

8.5.2.4

What Auditors Will Look For

■ Evidence that returned parts have been analyzed and that actions to prevent recurrence have been taken

8.5.3 PREVENTIVE ACTION

The organization must have a documented procedure that focuses on the prevention of problems before they occur. This is different from the corrective action procedure. Some organizations try to combine clauses 8.5.2 and 8.5.3; we do not recommend this. Preventive action is to be used to look for potential nonconformities in the QMS and customer products. The internal audit program and management reviews are excellent opportunities to look for preventive actions, but all personnel should be encouraged to look for potential improvements in the work that they do.

The recommended steps in a preventive action process must, at a minimum, include:

- Methods for determining potential nonconformities and root causes
- Methods for evaluating the need for such preventive actions, given such factors as costs, efficiencies, and timing
- Methods for planning and implementing ideas
- A system of record keeping
- Methods for ensuring that the preventive actions have worked as planned

---

8.5.3

What Auditors Will Look For

- Evidence that preventive action studies have been conducted and that actions have been taken to reduce potential problems
- Sources of information used for preventive actions
- How root cause determinations were made

SUMMARY

The measurement, analysis, and improvement section provides concepts that the organization must use to monitor, audit, control, correct, and prevent issues in the QMS. These items are critical for an organization to include in its management review process. Quickly identifying issues that have occurred and learning to prevent future issues is a key factor in long-term survival in the automotive supply base.

Note: Annex A of the control plan is covered in chapter 10.

Chapter Nine

Production Part Approval Process Requirements

I n the simplest terms, the production part approval process (PPAP) is used to verify that a newly tooled part, or a part modified by an engineering change, meets all engineering requirements and that various statistical tools have been used to increase the likelihood of a problem-free launch. PPAP is an ISO/TS 16949 requirement for suppliers to DaimlerChrysler, Ford, GM, and many tier-one suppliers.

There is a major misunderstanding by some suppliers that PPAP simply consists of filling out the so-called PPAP warrant. This is most certainly not the case. It is vital that you understand that filling out and signing the warrant without having conducted the required tests and finding that the test results show conformance with specifications constitutes fraud. Although we are not aware of existing prosecutions for such fraud, such prosecution is certainly conceivable.

PPAP resulted from the harmonization of DaimlerChrysler's, Ford's and GM's unique approaches for approving new and changed parts for shipment to the customer. The DaimlerChrysler and GM processes utilized customer and independent testing laboratories to verify conformance to specifications, while Ford used verification at the supplier's site by customer quality engineers. In the early 1990s, all three automakers had evolved to some level of supplier self-certification, but with vestiges of their earlier approaches. Prompted by supplier requests for a common part-approval process, representatives from the Big Three developed PPAP, the first body of harmonized requirements in the U.S. auto industry. It became effective in 1993, a year before the release of QS-9000, and it has been updated twice.

The PPAP manual should be read by every person in the supplier's organization connected in any way with the launch of new products and the incorporation of engineering changes to existing products. Like ISO/TS 16949, it is neither long nor difficult to understand. Integrity demands that supplier personnel comprehend what they are doing when their company completes a PPAP warrant.

A sentence early in the PPAP manual needs emphasis: "Any results that are outside specifications are cause for the supplier not to submit the parts, documentation, and/or records."

If out-of-specification results occur, the product must be corrected and the measurements and tests repeated. The only results that allow signing and submitting the warrant and any other required documentation is 100 percent conformance to specifications.

A further misunderstanding by some suppliers is that PPAP is all that is required for authority to begin shipping new or changed products. There are significant differences in the way that each OEM uses PPAP, and there may well be additional requirements unique to a particular customer. There are also differences between various divisions within a particular customer. It's not uncommon to find that powertrain divisions have different requirements than vehicle assembly operations. There may also be unique requirements for specific vehicle or powertrain programs. Please refer to PPAP Section II, Customer-Specific Requirements, or to your customer's purchasing group for details related to your part submission.

Manual Layout

The PPAP manual contains two sections and a group of appendices.

Section I covers the main requirements that all suppliers must fulfill:

- General
- PPAP process requirements
- Customer notification and submission requirements
- Submission to customer—levels of evidence
- Part submission status
- Record retention

Section II contains special requirements from DaimlerChrysler, Ford, GM, and the truck OEMs.

The appendix section contains:

- Completion of the part submission warrant
- Completion of the appearance approval report
- Dimensional report

- Material test report
- Performance test report
- Bulk material—specific requirements
- Tire industry—specific requirements

BOTTOM LINE

It's vital that a supplier's PPAP coordinator maintain close contact with each customer parts approval activity. If there is any doubt about whom to contact, the supplier's contact in the customer's purchasing function will be able to resolve the issue.

There are nineteen specific PPAP requirements. All of these requirements apply to every production part, component, or system supplied to customers' requirements. They also apply to bulk materials when specifically required by the customer. The only exception is that if the production part is not identified as an "appearance item" (generally, any product with color, grain, texture, or other appearance features), there is no requirement for the appearance item report.

Although all of the PPAP requirements are important, three (plus the appearance approval report, when applicable) are crucial to verifying that newly tooled products meet requirements:

- Dimensional measurement results
- Material test results
- Functional test results

These results, when in conformance with the design record and any engineering changes, indicate that the product does meet design intent. The remaining requirements help to ensure that ongoing production will continue to meet design intent.

Another aspect of the PPAP is submission level. Each specific customer will assign all suppliers a submission level. It's possible that various customers with various organizations (e.g., powertrain, assembly, vehicle divisions) will assign different submission levels to your company. It's also possible that products from one of your manufacturing locations might have a different submission level than other manufacturing locations. Further submission levels might vary from one vehicle or powertrain program to another. It's wise to verify the required submission level with the parts approval activity for each new product.

As the term implies, "submission level" merely indicates what documents are to be submitted to the customer. The submission level has no effect whatsoever on the completion of the eighteen or nineteen requirements. There is some confusion on this subject at certain suppliers. We have encountered suppliers that believe (or would like to believe) that because they have received a "submission level 1," they only need to fill out a warrant and send it to their customers. This approach is both a major nonconformance against ISO/TS 16949 (one which would immediately put their registration on probation) and, as mentioned previously, constitutes fraud.

For both supplier management of the PPAP process and to avoid nonconformances during registrar audits, it's important to have a complete file of all PPAP documentation in one location for each part (or other product). Files should be available for all parts currently under contract with an OEM, but auditors will generally focus on the most recently launched products.

Aside from meeting requirements, complete PPAP files are invaluable if problems ever occur. The dimensional, material, and functional test results are a vital reference point, against which measurements and tests on current production can be compared. In this way, it can be quickly determined if the supplier's product has changed from the level that was initially approved via PPAP.

Chapter Ten

Advanced Product Quality Planning and Control Plan

T he *Advanced Product Quality Planning and Control Plan* manual was first issued in June of 1994. It's still in its first edition, so any copy—white cover (first printing) or blue cover (second printing)—can be considered a current version. The book contains two primary sections: the APQP process and control plans. It was conceived of as two manuals and later combined into one book with the control plans section added as section 6. (There are blank forms in the back of the manual that suppliers have permission to use as needed.)

The original term for this overall process was advanced quality planning. The word "product" was added in an effort to emphasize the need to have the process engineers conduct the product and manufacturing design processes. The overall process consists of five basic phases, or timings. Many customers have more specific timing matrices that your organization will need to follow in working with your suppliers. In many cases, you will need to require your suppliers to follow an APQP process that aligns with yours to meet your customers' requirements.

OVERVIEW

The APQP manual was the first attempt by DaimlerChrysler, Ford, and GM to standardize the design and manufacturing processes. Prior to June 1994, each automaker had its own specific process. This required suppliers to have three independent methods in place if they were to work with each automaker. The many methods used by suppliers to meet the automaker's requirements prior to APQP served as the basis for the APQP manual. The APQP manual is intended to act as a guideline and is not a requirement that must be followed to the letter, as the *Production Part Approval Process* (PPAP) manual is. There are fifty-two identified items, plus the control plan, that suppliers need to consider when planning their own APQP process to satisfy customers.

Few suppliers apply APQP as it was intended. APQP should be approached, especially given the requirements in ISO/TS 16949, by having the organization plan a process that will satisfy customer wants, needs, and requirements. Some original equipment manufacturers (OEMs)/automakers do have reports that need to be submitted during the APQP process, but these are only reporting points where the OEM wants to see what the supplier is doing. The supplier should have an APQP process that is appropriate to its particular organization, resources, and staff.

INTRODUCTION

The APQP manual begins with an overview of the product quality planning cycle (see figure 10.1), which is a means of clarifying communications throughout the automotive supply chain. The three circles complete a loop, indicating that this should be an ongoing process. The inner circle shows the five phases of the APQP process, which is the basic outline of the manual. The next circle shows a generic product quality planning event, which any organization can modify to meet its specific needs. The outer circle is the standard W. Edwards Deming (or Walter Shewhart) plan-do-study-act cycle (or plan-do-check-act cycle), which represents how activities should be viewed in an ever-improving environment.

The introduction of the APQP manual details an explanation of the black box/gray box supplier concepts, which are either design responsible or not design responsible, respectively. The fundamentals of product quality planning covers these topics:

- Organizing the team
- Defining the scope
- Team-to-team
- Training
- Customer and supplier involvement
- Simultaneous engineering
- Control plans
- Concern resolution
- Product quality timing plan
- Plans relative to the timing chart (see figure 10.2)

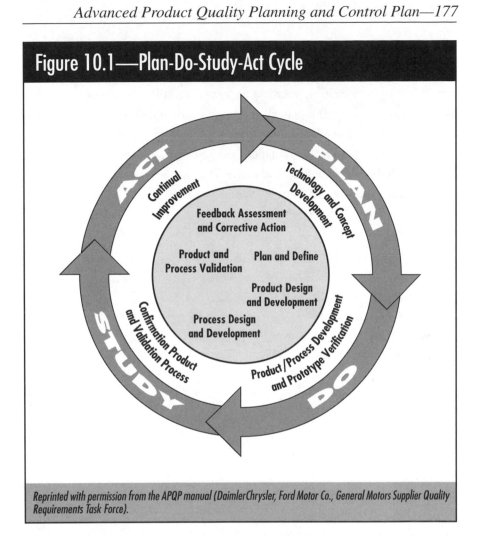

Figure 10.1—Plan-Do-Study-Act Cycle

Reprinted with permission from the APQP manual (DaimlerChrysler, Ford Motor Co., General Motors Supplier Quality Requirements Task Force).

The first five sections of the APQP manual list events that can be conducted during each of the suggested APQP timing phases. These are basic suggestions, developed by a team of suppliers and OEM personnel who studied the history of problems that occurred and decided what strategies might be used to prevent these problems in the future. Your organization may have some different views. Therefore, you should conduct your own risk analysis around your own particular APQP events, using the manual as a starting point.

Let's examine each section in turn.

1.0: PLAN AND DEFINE PROGRAM

In most organizations this is the first phase that product engineers will have to deal with. There are items described as "inputs" to this phase and other items described as "outputs." This is to represent the standard IPO (inputs, process, output), which demonstrates how information should flow through a system. Note that subsequent APQP phases do not list inputs because the outputs of the previous phase are considered the inputs of the next phase. This process uses all information and leaves nothing hanging as a nonvalue-adding process.

The inputs of the first phase include:

■ Voice of the customer
  ❏ Market research
  ❏ Historical warranty and quality information
  ❏ Team experience

■ Business plan/marketing strategy
■ Product/process benchmark data
■ Product/process assumptions
■ Product reliability studies
■ Customer inputs

The outputs of this phase include:

■ Design goals
■ Reliability and quality goals
■ Preliminary bill of material
■ Preliminary process flowchart
■ Preliminary listing of special product and process characteristics
■ Process assurance plan
■ Management support

2.0: PRODUCT DESIGN AND DEVELOPMENT

Each phase ends with the idea of management support and commitment. This is done intentionally. Many times when things go wrong, root causes usually include a lack of resources (or other information/materials) that were requested of management. To ensure customer satisfaction, top management must provide design teams with ongoing recognition and acknowledgment in product design and development.

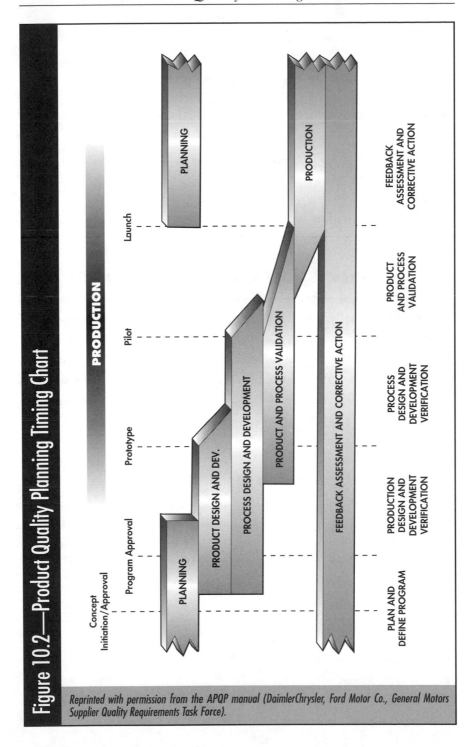

Figure 10.2—Product Quality Planning Timing Chart

Reprinted with permission from the APQP manual (DaimlerChrysler, Ford Motor Co., General Motors Supplier Quality Requirements Task Force).

The outputs of this phase include:

- Design failure mode and effects analysis (DFMEA)
- Design for manufacturability and design for assembly
- Design verification
- Design reviews
- Prototype build (control plan)
- Engineering drawings (including math data)
- Engineering specifications
- Material specifications
- Drawing and specification changes
- Management support

3.0: PROCESS DESIGN AND DEVELOPMENT

The manufacturing process must be designed and developed simultaneously with the product. Generally speaking, your customer has chosen your organization because you have previously produced something similar to the current product. This situation allows your company to use historical data in developing any new processes needed to make new parts. Caution should be used if you're asking your suppliers to produce items that are new to them. Planning the process becomes even more important if you or your supplier have never made this type of part before.

The outputs of this phase include:

- Packaging standards
- Product/process quality system review
- Process flowchart
- Floor plan layout
- Characteristics matrix
- Process failure mode and effects analysis (PFMEA)
- Pre-launch control plan
- Process instructions
- Measurement systems analysis plan
- Preliminary process capability study plan
- Packaging specifications
- Management support

4.0: PRODUCT AND PROCESS VALIDATION

A key factor in validation is ensuring that the products will be made in a way that satisfies not only the stated needs of the customers but also their unstated needs. Consider this comparison: If you go into a store to buy a watch, would you ask if the watch keeps accurate time? Few people do, because they assume that most watches will keep accurate time. The same thinking applies here; the products you deliver to your customers need to meet and exceed their expectations. (Another note: always test your products in true vehicle position, preferably on actual vehicles similar to those for which the product is intended. We've seen a number of failures caused by testing parts in ways other than how the parts will be used, causing unexpected failures.)

The outputs of this phase include:

■ Production trial run

■ Measurement systems evaluation

■ Preliminary process capability study

■ Production part approval

■ Production validation testing

■ Packaging evaluation

■ Production control plan

■ Quality planning sign-off

■ Management support

5.0: FEEDBACK, ASSESSMENT, AND CORRECTIVE ACTION

The final phase of the APQP process is to collect information for the next cycle. The challenge for many organizations is how to pass on this knowledge. As engineers move from job to job this becomes difficult. Often the person who knew about an existing problem is not associated with the next design project. We've heard again and again about failures that occurred because a new engineer didn't know about a problem that was found and fixed on an earlier process or design. To promote continual improvement, and to ensure that your customers are satisfied, your organization must find a way to pass on information from program to program.

The outputs of this phase, and the product that has been launched, should include:

■ Reduced variation

■ Customer satisfaction

Figure 10.3—Control Plan

	Prototype	Pre-launch	Production		Page ___ of ___

Control Plan Number		Key Contact/Phone	Date (Orig.)	Date (Rev.)
Part Number/Latest Change Level		Core Team	Customer Engineering Approval/Date (If Required)	
Part Name/Description		Supplier/Plant Approval/Date	Customer Quality Approval/Date (If Required)	
Supplier/Plant	Supplier code	Other Approval/Date (If Required)	Other Approval/Date (If Required)	

			Characteristics				Methods				
Part Process Number	Process Name/ Operation Description	Machine, Device, Jig, Tools for Mfg.	No.	Product	Process	Special Char. Class.	Product/ Process Specification/ Tolerance	Evaluation Measurement Technique	Sample		Control Method	Reaction Plan
									Size	Freq.		

Reprinted with permission from the APQP manual (DaimlerChrysler, Ford Motor Co., General Motors Supplier Quality Requirements Task Force).

- Delivery and service
- Management support

6.0: CONTROL PLAN DEVELOPMENT

As mentioned earlier, the control plan methodology is listed as section 6 in the APQP manual and is an output of the product and process validation phase of the APQP cycle. Control plans are tools used to summarize the parameters identified during the APQP process that need ongoing monitoring and verification during the production life of the part. The challenge is how to ensure that production parts meet customer requirements. The APQP manual provides the recommended form (see figure 10.3) and explains how each box on the form indicates what information should be listed. Each process should be analyzed for improvement opportunities. (This is commonly done with cause-and-effect diagrams.) This section also contains a number of supplemental examples for reference.

CHECKLISTS

The APQP and control plan teams that designed the manual also developed a series of checklists that should be used at various points in the design-and-development process. There is one error in the book that was not identified by the Automotive Industry Action Group (AIAG): page sixty-five, on the A-2 Design Information Checklist, item number seven. This item is not a repeat of number six and should read design for manufacturability and assembly.

Other checklists include:

- Design FMEA checklist
- New equipment, tooling, and test equipment checklist
- Product/process quality checklist
- Floor plan checklist
- Process flowchart checklist
- Process FMEA checklist
- Control plan checklist

OTHER ITEMS

The remainder of the manual consists of appendices, a glossary/acronym list, a bibliography, and blank forms, which are useful when designing a new product. The blank forms include two sign-off forms (Team Feasibility Commitment [E], and

Product Quality Planning Summary and Sign-Off [F]) that may be required by your customers.

SUMMARY

The *Advanced Product Quality Planning and Control Plan* manual was designed as a reference document. ISO/TS 16949 has several references (clauses 7.1.1, 7.5.1.2, and 8.1.1) that require the use of control plans or planning activities. Your organization must use a planning tool to help ensure that you are aware of customer requirements and that you are meeting and exceeding customer expectations. Control plans are required for prototype, for pre-launch, and during manufacturing. Overall, the APQP manual is a good overview of what your organization should be doing. The challenge for you is to use this manual in planning your company's own unique process.

Chapter Eleven

Potential Failure Mode and Effects Analysis

A ll suppliers to the U.S. Big Three are required to use the *Potential Failure Mode and Effects Analysis/FMEA, Third Edition,* manual to assist them in development of both design and process FMEAs. The FMEA manual states, "An FMEA can be described as a systematic group of activities intended to: (a) recognize and evaluate the potential failure of a product/process and the effects of that failure, (b) identify actions that could eliminate or reduce the chance of the potential failure occurring, and (c) document the entire process. It is complementary to the process of defining what a design or process must do to satisfy the customer."

Design and process FMEAs are a critical component of the advanced product quality planning (APQP) process that DaimlerChrysler, Ford, and GM require for planning and development of quality management systems (QMSs). DaimlerChrysler specifically requires the use of the APQP manual, whereas Ford requires its use as a guide in meeting Ford's APQP reporting guidelines. GM also requires that the APQP manual be used as a guide for meeting its global APQP.

Some 80 percent of the organizations that are registered to QS-9000 complain about the resources, time, and money they are required to spend (not invest) on non-value-adding tasks and programs to maintain their registration. These people evidently believe that it's more profitable for the company to do product and process design changes at prototype, pilot, and during regular production. They believe in funding a QMS that is focused on detection, which includes end-of-line inspection that is backed up by an "enhanced inspection area" (level one containment). This method also includes product rework areas, inspection, and the most inefficient of all, level two containment, where the customer experiencing continued quality spills (for which design failure is usually the root cause), requires the supplier to send the discrepant product to a third party, which doesn't understand the customer's requirements, to do what the supplier is unable to. With this approach, planned and preventive maintenance schedules are typically canceled due to the need to make up production due to scrap and rework. Premium freight (or "expediting") is a necessity rather than a QMS failure indicator. These suppliers believe that customers change their minds all the time anyway so it's easier to allocate resources for corrective action rather than spend the time and energy to prevent issues that may not even arise.

So why is it that 20 percent of the organizations have "gained" from their QS-9000 registration? These companies will tell you that they either already understood and/or followed QS-9000. They focus their resources on the product and process development process to ensure that product and process problems are identified, to predict their effect on production and the customer, and to develop and test changes and methods to identify and, where possible, prevent the occurrences before the design is accepted and passed on to the feasibility stage.

The basic developmental sequence (see figure 11.1) of any FMEA starts with asking, "What are the functions, features, or requirements?" The team should then ask, "What can go wrong?" This is followed by identifying the effect(s) and cause(s) and asking, "How can this problem be prevented and detected?" The identification of the cause and effect and the final question lead in selecting a numerical score that is used for severity, occurrence, and detection (respectively). The FMEA manual contains suggested numerical tables that a supplier should use to establish a base point for its operations. The three scores are then multiplied together to create a risk priority number (RPN). The RPN numbers can then be used in a Pareto chart to identify which issues should be addressed, and in what order.

Management teams that have ensured that their FMEA processes have enough time and resources available to complete this task have found many benefits and positive results in customer satisfaction and increased business. Note that the use of the RPN should not be used as an evaluation tool between FMEA projects. They are only to be used by the team working on a specific FMEA to look for areas of continual improvement of customer satisfaction.

DESIGN FMEA

The design FMEA is used to improve the design-and-development process. It's a process where the design-responsible engineer—along with a group of knowledge-

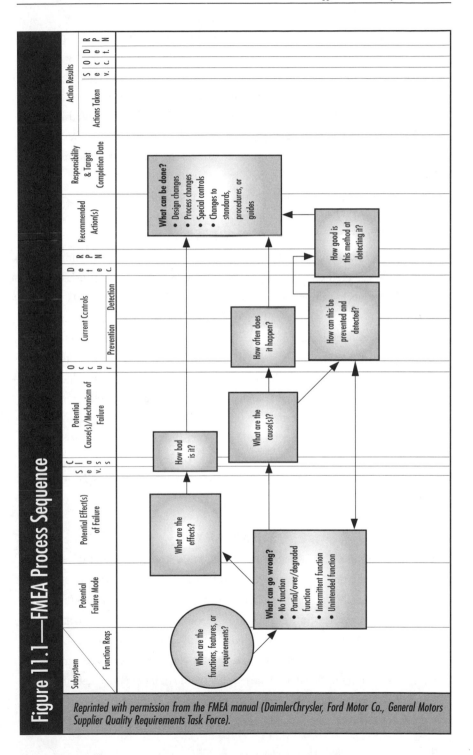

Figure 11.1—FMEA Process Sequence

Reprinted with permission from the FMEA manual (DaimlerChrysler, Ford Motor Co., General Motors Supplier Quality Requirements Task Force).

able individuals who represent the disciplines, components, and internal and external customers of the organization's product realization process—review and analyze all aspects of the product design and the known, perceived, and possible effects on tooling development, process development, manufacturing, warranty, campaigns, and future design-and-development programs. The FMEA's disciplined approach to analyzing all aspects of the design and ranking the severity of the effects on the rest of the design-and-development process allows top management to review the risks/cost and put action plans in place to eliminate and/or reduce the severity of effects before tooling and equipment specifications are finalized.

PROCESS FMEA

The process FMEA is used to improve the manufacturing process and focus on mistake-proofing methods. It's a process where the manufacturing/assembly-responsible engineer—along with a group of knowledgeable individuals who represent the disciplines, components, and internal and external customers of the organization's product design and process development process—review and analyze all aspects of the manufacturing and assembly processes to ensure that product and process problems were identified, to predict their effect on production and the customer, and to develop and test changes and methods to identify and, where possible, prevent the occurrences before the feasibility stage. This process allows top management to identify special and common cause problems and occurrences that can have a negative effect on pre-launch activities and, after start of production, to determine the severity and risk, and to identify error-/mistake-proofing solutions to minimize the their effect.

SUMMARY

Design and process FMEAs are not processes that stop the product-development process. "Fast to market" is essential in today's global economy. With the right people representing all the appropriate disciplines of the design and manufacturing system, the common and special cause occurrences that plague the organization after the start of production can be identified and solutions applied to minimize their effect on quality, schedule, and cost. FMEAs are living documents that, when updated as new information is identified during the production life of the product, help the organization avoid the same negative effects in future product realization programs.

See the DaimlerChrysler, Ford, and GM *Potential Failure Mode and Effects Analysis, Third Edition,* manual, available through your OEM or the Automotive Industry Action Group, for detailed information.

Chapter Twelve

Statistical Process Control

T he *Statistical Process Control* (SPC) reference manual was released in the fall of 1992, and its cover was updated in 1995. The SPC development team states that the manual, "… should be considered an introduction to statistical process control. It is not intended to limit evolution of statistical methods suited to particular processes or commodities, nor is it intended to be comprehensive of all SPC techniques." In fact, the only current SPC tools discussed in the manual are control charts, also called process behavior charts.

The history of control charts goes back to the 1920s and the work of Walter Shewhart, often called the father of modern quality control.

The SPC manual is divided into four chapters, covering: an introduction to continual improvement, charts for variables, charts for attributes, and an overview of measurement analysis techniques. The bulk of the text is found in chapters 2 and 3, which deal with the charts themselves.

In this chapter, we will give a quick overview of the SPC reference manual without getting into the details of constructing control charts. You should review these basic tools to see which apply to your organization's needs. Control charts are used to show stability in a process, which is different than working toward continual improvement of a process. Stability does not necessarily equal improvement.

INTRODUCTION TO CONTINUAL IMPROVEMENT AND SPC

The SPC reference manual design team intended the manual to be used by practitioners and managers as an introduction to, or a review of, statistical methods. They list six points that need to be understood as a foundation to the overall concept of continual improvement:

■ Gathering data and using statistical methods to interpret them are not ends in themselves.

■ The concept of studying variation and using statistical signals to improve performance can be applied to any area.

■ The focus should be on the process.

■ Real understanding of SPC involves deep contact with the actual processes in your organization and attempts to control those situations.

■ The SPC reference manual should be used as the first step toward the use of statistical methods.

■ Measurement systems are critical to proper data analysis and must be understood before process data are collected.

The first chapter contains a review of the concepts of:

■ Prevention vs. detection—everything can be defined in terms of a process (see figure 12.1) using the inputs-process-outputs concepts that are currently being used in the ISO 9001:2000 process model

■ How to identify common cause (random/controlled) and special cause (sporadic/uncontrolled) variation

■ The difference between local actions and actions on the system (which involve management)

■ The necessity of making economically sound decisions about what is done in a process by studying the processes and process capability

■ Using the plan-do-study-act cycle to analyze, maintain, and improve the process

■ The basic foundations of how to use control charts (covered in detail in chapters 2 and 3 of the manual)

■ The benefits of using control charts

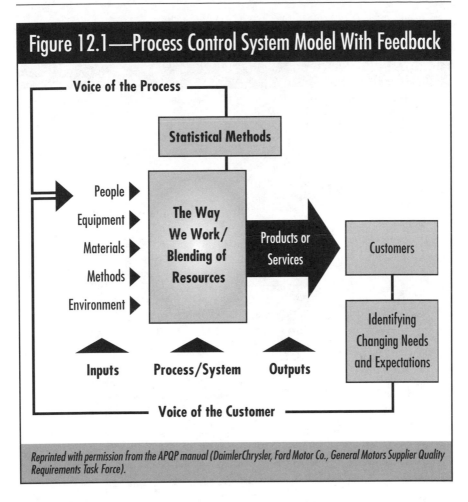

Figure 12.1—Process Control System Model With Feedback

Voice of the Process

Statistical Methods

People ▶
Equipment ▶
Materials ▶
Methods ▶
Environment ▶

The Way We Work/ Blending of Resources

Products or Services

Customers

Identifying Changing Needs and Expectations

▲ **Inputs**   ▲ **Process/System**   ▲ **Outputs**

Voice of the Customer

Reprinted with permission from the APQP manual (DaimlerChrysler, Ford Motor Co., General Motors Supplier Quality Requirements Task Force).

Chapter 1 covers the foundations of what we call modern quality assurance, using control charts to help manage processes. The selection of the appropriate chart can be seen in the figure at the front of the SPC manual or in its appendix C (see figure 12.2).

Figure 12.2—Selection Procedure for the Use of Control Charts

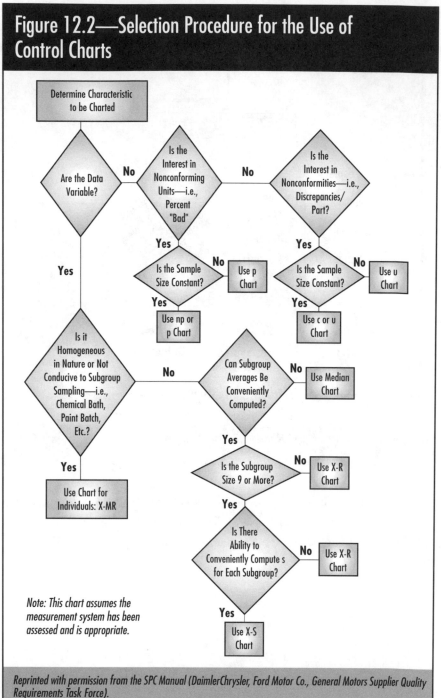

Note: This chart assumes the measurement system has been assessed and is appropriate.

CONTROL CHARTS FOR VARIABLES

Chapter 2 of the SPC manual deals with the charts most commonly used with variables (linear measurements—quantitative values) data. The use of charts for variable data is useful in the quest to monitor and prevent problems. This is so for several reasons:

Charts can be used in nearly all processes, because outputs can typically be measured.

Quantitative values contain more information than qualitative values.

■ Charts provide more overall information for the number of parts that need to be checked, resulting in lower overall measurement costs.

■ Charts provide a quicker decision-making process over attribute data, resulting in a favorable time gap to decision.

■ Charts can provide data to be analyzed, even if the parts are within specification, to continually improve the process.

One reason that variables process behavior charts (control charts) are so powerful is the nature of the data collection process itself. Data gathered in the variable process can be divided into two types of information: spread (piece-to-piece variability) and location (process average). Using this information, the operator can tell if the process variation is holding the same, increasing, or decreasing, and, at the same time, be able to tell if the process is deviating from the target for the product. This pairing of information (commonly used in X bar and R charts) can show how the process is behaving under normal operating conditions and indicate if actions need to be taken to maintain control or to identify if improvements are needed.

Chapter 2 of the SPC manual goes into detail on the foundations of variable charting and is divided into five sections:

■ Average and range charts
■ Average and standard deviation charts
■ Median charts
■ Charts for individuals and moving range
■ How to understand the use of process capability with process performance of variables data

These sections cover the basic techniques of how to construct the charts and how to use them on the shop floor. The use of these charts should aid the operator in

Figure 12.3—Control Chart

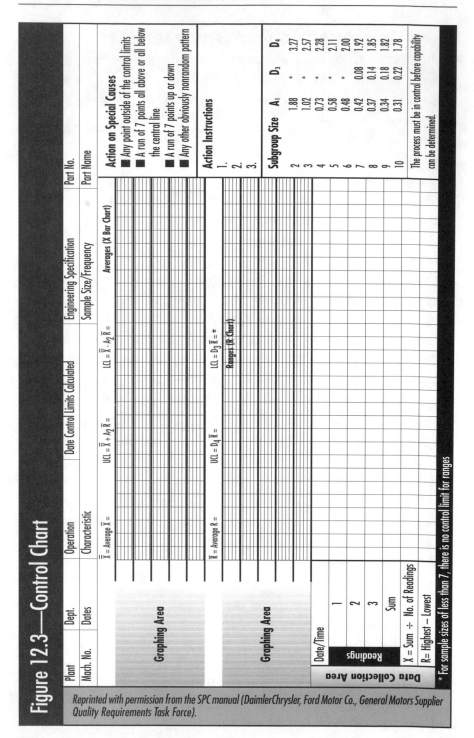

Reprinted with permission from the SPC manual (DaimlerChrysler, Ford Motor Co., General Motors Supplier Quality Requirements Task Force).

evaluating if the process is running within normal statistical boundaries—i.e., the process is in control.

Section one deals with how to construct average and range charts. To begin the process, an organization should take the following steps:

1. Establish an environment suitable for action
2. Define the process
3. Determine characteristics to be charted
4. Define the measurement system
5. Minimize unnecessary variation

After each of these steps is taken, the data can be collected and construction of the chart can begin once the subgroup size, frequency, and number is determined. Forms typically used for plotting this data (see figure 12.3) have two areas for plotting points and a data collection area. Once the desired number of subgroups has been collected (typically twenty five), calculations and constants can be used to determine the averages and control limits for the process in question.

The interpretation of the charts can then be determined by watching the patterns of the data on the graphs. Operators, engineers, supervisors, and managers can develop their chart-reading skills over time by using the charts to make predictions about the behavior of the process. Some of the ways that the charts can show that the process is changing include:

■ One point falling outside of the plus/minus 3 sigma control limit
■ Seven successive points on the same side of the centerline
■ Seven successive points that either increase or decrease
■ Two out of three successive points that are both on the same side of the centerline and outside of the plus/minus 2 sigma zone
■ Four of five successive points that are on the same side of the centerline and outside of the plus/minus 1 sigma zone
■ Other nonrandom patterns, such as trends, cycles, or an unusual spread of points within the control limits

Once the process has been determined to be in control, the capability of the process can be determined. With this information, you can be certain that as long as the process remains in control, you will have the same capability as that of your stated study. This is true because a process that is statistically in control is a stable process. You

Figure 12.4—Control Chart for Attribute Data

Plant	❑ p ❑ c ❑ np ❑ u	Part Number and Name	
Department	Operation Number and Name		

Ave. =	UCL =	LCL=	Date Control Limits Calculated	Average Sample Size:	Frequency:

Graphing Area

	Sample (n)	
Discrepancies	Number (np, c)	
	Proportion (p, u)	Data Collection Area
	Date (Shift, Time, etc.)	

Any change in people, equipment, materials, methods, environment, or measurement systems, should be noted. These notes will help you to take corrective or process improvement action when signaled by the control chart.

Date	Time	Comments

Reprinted with permission from the SPC manual (DaimlerChrysler, Ford Motor Co., General Motors Supplier Quality Requirements Task Force).

can be certain that nothing is changing that will affect the overall output of the process. Note that this state does not provide evidence of a continually improving process. It just demonstrates that the process is stable.

CONTROL CHARTS FOR ATTRIBUTES

Chapter 3 of the SPC manual deals with charts for qualitative data: good/bad, yes/no, go/no-go. The most common of these include the p chart (proportion of units nonconforming), the np chart (number of units nonconforming), the c chart (number of nonconformities), and the u chart (number of nonconformities per unit). The benefits commonly associated with such attribute charts include:

■ Any technical or administrative process can be described using attributes data.

■ Many processes already collect some form of attribute information, so collecting the data will not be an extra expense.

■ Attribute information is usually inexpensive and can be gathered quickly.

■ Many managerial reports already use attribute type data and would benefit from using control chart analysis techniques.

■ When used to assist in pinpointing areas for improvement, attribute charts can give a broad view, helping management decide where more detailed analysis is needed.

The four sections of chapter 3 of the SPC manual cover the details of how to construct each of the attribute charts, which includes gathering data and calculating the control limits. The methods for interpreting the data are then briefly discussed, as this is similar to the variable data interpretation. For process capability studies using attribute data, the chapter defines capability as the average proportion or rate of nonconforming product.

PROCESS MEASUREMENT SYSTEM ANALYSIS

Chapter 4 of the SPC manual provides a basic overview of another core tool book called *Measurement System Analysis* (MSA). The reader can use this chapter as an overview or use the actual MSA manual as a starting point for conducting gage studies to ensure that your measurement system is behaving in a way that will deliver the planned results.

SUMMARY

Control charts provide an early indication that something has changed or that a problem is about to happen. Using a computer or other method of calculating the data does little if someone doesn't take action in response to the signals that charts present. The challenge is for organizations to use such charts to understand both when things are running well and when changes are needed to maintain the stability of the process.

Chapter Thirteen

Measurement Systems Analysis

The Big Three first released the *Measurement Systems Analysis* (MSA) manual in 1990, with follow-up editions in 1995 and 2002. The base material for this manual was generated from work done primarily by GM. Through the three editions, there has consistently been a push for suppliers to look at their measurement systems and reduce the variation of measurement error. The third edition is the most detailed of the series and now mandates a number of actions that were mentioned in previous editions, but rarely done.

In the third edition, suppliers must identify families of gages and, for at least one production gage from each family, conduct stability studies (control charts), bias, linearity, and full gage repeatability and reproducibility (GR&R) with an array of graphical analysis studies. Although these studies require significant time, they are an investment that will pay dividends by providing trustworthy input for process control and problem solving. It's management's responsibility to provide the appropriate resources. They should be aware that these studies are not just a cost of doing business but a foundation for competent process management.

The MSA manual is divided into five main chapters, with chapter 3 detailing the main requirements for variable gage studies (see figure 13.1). Attribute studies are required, but are still limited by the technology available to understand how attribute gages operate. In addition to the five chapters, there are a number of appendixes and a reference list for future study. One item of note is reference thirteen on page 211, which lists Richard Gillespie's book, *Manufacturing Knowledge: A History of the Hawthorne Experiments* (Cambridge University Press, 1991). This is a well-written summary of the famous experiments conducted by Elton Mayo at Western Electric's Hawthorne Works in Chicago from 1927 to 1932. An understanding of

Figure 13.1—Measurement Systems Analysis Third Edition Quick Guide

Type of Measurement System	MSA Methods	Chapter
Basic Variable	Range, Average & Range, ANOVA, Bias, Linearity, Control Charts	III
Basic Attribute	Signal Detection, Hypothesis Test Analyses	III
Nonreplicable (e.g., Destructive Tests)	Control Charts	IV
Complex Variable	Range, Average & Range, ANOVA, Bias, Linearity, Control Charts	III, IV
Multiple Systems, Gages, or Test Stands	Control Charts, ANOVA, Regression Analysis	III, IV
Continuous Process	Control Charts	III
Miscellaneous	Alternate Approaches	V
Other	White Papers—available at www.aiag.org/publications/quality/msa2.html	

Reprinted with permission from the MSA manual (DaimlerChrysler, Ford Motor Co., General Motors Supplier Quality Requirements Task Force).

the Hawthorne Studies is recommended for those conducting blind evaluator tests. Such an understanding will help ensure that inspector attitudes are keep to a minimum during the inspection process.

GENERAL MEASUREMENT SYSTEM GUIDELINES

MSA's chapter 1 contains seven sections that cover the basics of what a measurement system should include. One of the primary reasons for conducting an MSA should be to ensure that the benefit derived from using measurement data is great enough to warrant the cost of obtaining it. This requires that attention be focused on the quality of the data. Many organizations have reduced production variation over the last twenty years. Now it's time to work on measurement error variation.

After giving some basic definitions, the MSA manual addresses a measurement system variability cause-and-effect diagram. This concept should be expanded for your organization and divided by gage families, as external auditors could ask for evidence of a gage plan for the plant. Top management can use the cause-and-effect diagram as a tool to identify how gages are used and to what extent measurement error is being addressed.

The chapter continues with discussions about gage source selection, further planning, and a checklist entitled: "Suggested Elements for a Measurement System Development Checklist." This checklist should be a starting point for top management to review how MSA is conducted at your plant.

The chapter ends with a discussion of measurement issues. Many of the reasons why the OEMs felt that a third edition of the MSA manual was required are discussed here. The main reason is because many supplier organizations were not meeting or exceeding customer expectations. This section starts off by stating that measurement systems must demonstrate adequate sensitivity and be stable.

One major note that has been added here states, "The long-standing tradition of reporting measurement error only as a percent of tolerance is inadequate for the challenges of the marketplace which emphasize strategic and continuous process improvement." Top managers must realize that things are not business as usual anymore. Registrars look for MSA systems that meet the demands of this third edition, which is required in ISO/TS 16949:2002's clause 7.6.1, Measurement system analysis.

Although the "gage family" concept is generally recognized and acceptable, it can lead to shortcuts that miss significant sources of measurement error. In one of the authors' experience, there was evidence of large differences in measurement error across a gage family in actual use. In that particular plant, the decision was made to abandon the family concept and to do a separate study on each gage. Certainly when the process capability is marginal, each gage should be studied, as it is not unknown for poor Cpks to have a large component of measurement error that, when reduced, make an apparently noncapable process capable.

GENERAL CONCEPTS FOR ASSESSING MEASUREMENT SYSTEMS

MSA's chapter 2 begins with an overview of phase one and phase two testing. Phase one testing verifies that the correct variable(s) are being measured at the proper characteristic locations, as per the measurement system design specifications. Phase two testing studies the gage as it is being used over a long period of time, to ensure its stability.

The next three sections of chapter 2 cover selecting/developing the test procedures, preparing for a measurement study, and the analysis of the study results. In the third edition, as in earlier manuals, the general rule of thumb for measurement system acceptability is:

■ Less than 10 percent error—considered acceptable

■ 10 to 30 percent error—may be acceptable depending on customer needs, importance of the characteristic being measured, cost of measurement devices, and other factors

■ More than 30 percent error—unacceptable; every effort should be made to improve the measurement system

Care should be used in setting up and conducting measurement studies, as we have seen situations where, due to a poorly run measurement system analysis, a management team has spent a lot of time and money trying to fix problems that didn't exist.

A new item in the third edition is the calculation of the number of distinct categories (NDC). The NDC is used to reliably distinguish if the number of categories in the measurement system will ensure an overall accurate study. Using the constant provided on the form, the resulting value should be greater than five.

RECOMMENDED PRACTICES FOR SIMPLE MEASUREMENT SYSTEMS

The assumptions to be used in working with MSA's chapter 3 on variables or attributes include:

■ Only the three factors of appraisers, parts, and measurement system repeatability are to be studied.

■ Variability within each part is considered very small.

■ No statistical interactions can be found between the appraisers and the parts.

■ The parts do not change dimensionally during the study.

Given these assumptions, which are considered normal for gage studies, the organization can proceed with the variable and attribute studies. There is considerably more detail required for the variable studies than in past editions of MSA. Basically, an organization must now conduct studies around stability, bias, and linearity for each gage family, in addition to the GR&R study of the past.

To conduct a stability study, the organization must identify one gage or instrument for each gage family and conduct a control chart on that piece of equipment. The frequency of the study is to be daily or weekly, depending on factors that the organization identifies, and timing of the checks is to be representative of actual production operations. This will give an indication of how stable the measurement system is in the daily production system.

To conduct a bias study, a part must be chosen and measured by a coordinate measuring machine or other highly sophisticated methods a minimum of ten times, to establish a reference value for the characteristics to be studied. An appraiser (operator, inspector, or other user of the equipment) must then measure the part between 10 and 30 times. Analyzing the average and standard deviation of the appraiser as compared to the reference value will give an indication of how well the measurement system is performing to intended needs of the organization. Instruments that may not be measuring true can still be used if the bias is known and taken into consideration when checking parts. Also, the MSA manual discusses a range method for calculating bias.

Linearity looks at the bias of an instrument over the range or scale of the gage. It has been found that some instruments have a tendency to wear after being used to measure the same part for extended periods. These situations need to be identified and understood to ensure that customer requirements are being met. In most cases, the organization will need to use software to perform the calculations and graphical analysis needed for this study. There is also a range method for calculating linearity.

GR&R has been used for a number of years and is generally well-understood. However, there is now the need to use a number of graphical analysis tools in conjunction with the GR&R to better understand what the forms are indicating. Also, the constants that have been traditionally used on the GR&R report were based on 5.15 sigma. The MSA third edition has changed the constants to be in line with 6 sigma. The message is clear. The measurement system requirements are being tightened so that suppliers (engineering, manufacturing, and quality) will take more time in understanding the gage systems that are being used in their facilities.

The attribute gage study remains basically the same, as little research has yet been done to improve the techniques used to improve the attribute systems. Suppliers should continue to collect large-scale data sets to conduct the attribute gage studies.

PRACTICES FOR COMPLEX MEASUREMENT SYSTEMS

When the assumptions of chapter 3 are not true, then alternative methods for studying measurement systems must be found. MSA's chapter 4 reviews destructive testing and systems where the part actually changes. Fourteen options are given for the engineer to work with, depending on whether the process is stable or based on the nature of the testing itself. Additional references are listed to allow the engineer to look for better methods of conducting measurement systems analysis.

OTHER MEASUREMENT CONCEPTS

MSA's chapter 5 essentially pulls the appendixes of the second edition into the main text. There are techniques and information that the system analyzer should take into consideration, depending on the system being studied. Organizations are expected to review this section to look for applications information for their plant environment.

SUMMARY

If you only do what the MSA second edition called for in your organization, your registrar will probably issue a major nonconformance in your ISO/TS 16949:2002 audit. Managers must review the new requirements in the MSA third edition and make resources and time available to conduct the studies that are needed. For variable gage families these studies are: stability, bias, linearity, and graphical analysis in conjunction with the GR&R. The focus on gage families is to spur organizations to study areas where gages may be unreliable. To continually reduce variation, a gage system must be capable of giving accurate information.

Chapter Fourteen

IAOB-IATF Infrastructure

U nder QS-9000, suppliers relied on the Supplier Quality Requirements Task Force (SQRTF) for guidance and direction in dealing with questions related to the QS-9000 requirements. With the global application of ISO/TS 16949:2002, a globalized group was needed to offer the same direction that was given under QS-9000. This group is the International Automotive Task Force (IATF) and is made up of the SQRTF as well as representatives from the European automotive organizations, as discussed in chapter 1.

The IATF has developed three companion documents for ISO/TS 16949:2002:

■ Quality Management System Assessment Check-List Based on Process Approach Audit (also known the Checklist to ISO/TS 16949:2002)
■ IATF Guidance to ISO/TS 16949:2002
■ IATF Automotive Certification Scheme for ISO/TS 16949:2002, Rules for Achieving IATF Recognition

We will examine each of these documents, touching upon what they contain and how your organization should use them to ensure that you and your registrar are meeting ISO/TS 16949's requirements. The goal of these three documents, in conjunction with ISO/TS 16949 and customer-specific requirements, is to assist organizations in achieving continual improvement in meeting customer requirements and thereby customer satisfaction.

IATF CHECKLIST TO ISO/TS 16949:2002

This document contains two chapters. Chapter 1 of the checklist is designed to give additional explanation of what the process approach to auditing entails.

ISO 9001:1994 was based on an element compliance model, which was conducive to element-based auditing and the use of prescriptive checklists. QS-9000 enhanced that approach and began the movement toward what is now called the process approach. The checklist is not necessarily the most effective tool, but it does provide guidance to the auditor (external or internal) in ensuring that all aspects of ISO/TS 16949 are being met.

Chapter 2 of the checklist is a clause-by-clause review of the requirements and the recommended assessment items for an audit. The foreword to the checklist states: "The 'what to look for' column is not mandatory, but it is a good guide. It is expected that auditors will supplement this column with their educated and experienced enhancements."

You should expand the checklist to include items that are critical and unique to your organization's business. Furthermore, whenever customer problems or internal issues are found to relate to shortcomings in the quality management system (QMS), appropriate items should be added to your checklist.

IATF GUIDANCE TO ISO/TS 16949:2002

This document was written to provide guidance in the application of ISO/TS 16949:2002. It's to be used for reference only and not as a standard. Automotive suppliers are directed to consult various Web sites, including *www.iaob.org*, to keep up to date with the changing materials for ISO/TS 16949:2002.

The guidance document covers all the primary clauses in ISO/TS 16949:2002. In many cases the statements, "No further IATF guidance on this ISO 9001:2000 clause," or "No further IATF guidance on this automotive requirements clause," are offered. Otherwise, guidance is offered as to what the IATF would like suppliers and registrars to be aware of in ISO/TS 16949:2002, including ISO 9001:2000.

The last item in the guidance document is a checklist of items that an organization seeking ISO/TS 16949:2002 registration should submit to its registrar or certification body. This information includes:

- Organization size
- Site to be certified
- Supporting locations (if any)
- Product design responsibility (if any)
- Certification scope (What does your organization want to be known for?)
- Organization's processes—descriptions including sequence and interactions

(Commonly, copies of the turtle diagrams, octopus diagrams, and high-level process flow maps are a minimum submission.)

■ Key indicator trends (last twelve months) (At a minimum, organizations should provide data on customer satisfaction, employee motivation or awareness studies, product realization process analysis, and supplier performance indicators.)

■ Internal audit results and action plans (last twelve months) (What has the internal audit processes found and what actions have been taken?)

■ Management review results (last twelve months) (What has been identified in the management review cycle and what actions have been taken?)

■ Customer complaint status (A quick check in the organization's shipping department may provide a list of items that need to be addressed.)

■ Internal auditor qualifications (as outlined in the standard)

■ Customer-specific requirements to be included in the audit (Currently, only DaimlerChrysler, Ford, and GM customer-specific requirements are posted on the IAOB Web site. There is some discussion of posting tier-one customer's requirements in the future. Your organization must identify all of your customer-specific needs that relate to the scope of your audit and provide this information to the registrar.)

■ Current certifications held

■ Quality manual (You may want to send an uncontrolled copy to your registrar for reference. Frequently, the quality manual will be included in the readiness review.)

Note that in cases where data are being requested, the typical requirement is for twelve months of information. A number of suppliers have been caught by this requirement (as there is nothing this specific in ISO/TS 16949:2002 itself) and have found that they cannot be audited until the data become available. This could cause an issue for your organization if you are facing a customer deadline for becoming registered and you have yet to start collecting the required data. However, data that were collected under the supplier's previous QMS will meet these requirements.

IATF RULES

This document is mostly aimed at registrars and at auditors who work for registrars. Only IATF-approved registrars can conduct formal ISO/TS 16949:2002 registrations. Accreditation of a registrar by a national accreditation body such as the

American National Standards Institute-Registrar Accreditation Board National Accreditation Program (ANSI-RAB NAP) or the Standards Council of Canada does not confer acceptability for ISO/TS 16949:2002 registrations. It's important to note that not all accredited registrars have been approved by the IATF for ISO/TS 16949:2002 registrations. (See appendix A for a current list of IATF-approved registrars.)

The IATF rules document contains a number of mandatory requirements for registrars and lead auditors that must be followed for an ISO/TS 16949:2002 registration to be valid. Organizations seeking registration should be aware of these requirements. This will enable them to ask the appropriate questions of prospective registrars. What follows is a summary of the rules document.

1. Certification Body (CB)

ISO/TS 16949:2002 registrars are prevented from conducting any form of consulting activities with an auditee for a period of two years prior to the registration audit. This includes conducting no more than one pre-audit per organization site. The only exception to this rule are public courses offered by registrars. If your organization wishes to have a pre-assessment or gap analysis done prior to your registrar's visit, you must hire a second registrar or consulting firm that is capable of conducting an ISO/TS 16949:2002 audit.

However, in most cases the readiness review conducted by your registrar will identify any areas that might cause nonconformances during registration. Even if nonconformances are found during registration, it is generally more cost and time effective to avoid a separate pre-assessment and proceed directly to the readiness review and the actual registration audit. Bear in mind that any nonconformances identified during the registration audit won't stop the audit (unless the client requests it). Also, remember that nonconformances don't require a complete new audit, only an audit of the area affected by the nonconformance.

2. Audit Process

Registrars must follow a prescribed format for conducting audits. This process is closely monitored by the IATF, which conducts unannounced witness audits on registrars as they audit clients. A flowchart of the process is listed in annex 1 of the rules document and does indicate that the management of the auditee must ensure that a readiness audit is conducted before the registrar conducts the formal audit.

Registration to ISO/TS 16949:2002 is not allowed if any minor or major non-conformities are found. The definitions for nonconformities are:

■ *Major nonconformity*—presence of one or more of the following:
  ❏ Absence or total breakdown of a system to meet a requirement
  ❏ Any noncompliance that would result in the probability of shipping noncon-forming product to the customer
  ❏ A nonconformance that in the judgment or experience of the auditor would likely lead to a failure of the QMS

■ *Minor nonconformity*—a failure in the QMS, or a single observed lapse, that would in the judgment or experience of the auditor not lead to a failure of the QMS, but could reduce the ability to assure controlled processes or products

For organizations that are currently registered, a customer complaint or a non-conformity in a follow-up audit can cause the organization's registration to be put into the decertification process outlined in annex 4. For corporate certificates, if one site in the organization becomes decertified, then *all* sites within that corporation also lose their registration to ISO/TS 16949:2002. As a result, many multi-plant organizations forgo the modest savings allowed by a corporate registration plan and obtain separate registrations for each plant.

All audits conducted at the site (internal or surveillance) must review the following items:

■ Any new customers since the last audit (requirements, process requirements, etc.)
■ Any customer complaints and the organization's response to such complaints
■ The results and resulting actions of the organization's internal audit and management review
■ The organization's progress toward meeting continual improvement targets
■ The effectiveness measures of corrective actions and verifications made since the last audit

All audits plans must include an evaluation of the entire QMS and the effective implementation of ISO/TS 16949:2002. The assessment reports must include an evaluation of:

- The effectiveness of the system (using the process model that starts with customer requirements and ends with customer satisfaction)
- Process linkages
- The system's performance (results metrics) as compared to the management business plan
- The system requirements achieved
- A review of one complete internal audit and management review cycle

3. Audit Team

When the auditors from a registrar arrive to conduct an ISO/TS 16949:2002 audit, there are certain requirements that must be met. One example of these requirements is auditor competence. At least one of the auditors should be the same person during any three-year cycle; the registrar must evaluate the auditors; an audit report is due to you within fifteen days; and witness audit provisions are due within your contract with the registrar.

The organization cannot refuse an IATF witness audit of the certification body. This allows the IATF to arrive (possibly unannounced) during an audit to verify that the registrar is conducting the audit according to procedures. Witness audits are a critique of the registrar's practices and will normally have no effect on your assessment's results or the way that it is conducted.

4. Other Requirements

There are some additional rules that registrars must follow. For example, consultants you hire are not allowed to participate in the audits; registrars are expected to follow all rules and respect the IATF's and ISO's copyrights. Only the IATF can approve registrars to conduct ISO/TS 16949:2002 audits (see appendix A), and certificates are only good for a maximum of three years. A matrix of audit days has been developed for organizations and registrars to follow in transitioning from various standards to ISO/TS 16949:2002. Your registrar will work with you on your unique circumstances to meet the requirements.

If your organization ever decides to change its registrar, a specified sequence of steps must take place:

1. The new registrar must be approved by the IATF.
2. You must have a current ISO/TS 16949:2002 registration. (In other words, you cannot change registrars if your company has been decertified.)

3. The new registrar must review the most recent audit report and all findings of the previous registrar.
4. A formal document review of your system, as well as a review of the key performance indicators of your QMS, must take place.
5. A conversion audit must be conducted to finish out the current registration cycle (or a re-certification audit, if the change occurs at the end of a current registration cycle).
6. The new registrar must notify IATF of the change.
7. The rules document must be followed.

The IATF will monitor all activities to ensure that the registrars are adhering to all rules and requirements.

5. ISO/TS 16949:2002 Certificate Content Requirements

Registrars can modify the appearance of the ISO/TS 16949:2002 certificate that organizations receive; however, there are rules concerning what must be included on the actual certificate. Registrars are not allowed to reference documents that they are not accredited or recognized for.

6. Forms and Tables

Registrars are required to submit reports to the IATF on a regular basis using the specified formats listed in this section.

Annex 1. Rules for Auditing Quality Management Systems According to ISO/TS 16949:2002

A matrix has been created listing the sequence of activities that a registrar must follow in conducting audits for ISO/TS 16949:2002. The areas covered are activities before the audit, audit planning, site audit and reports, nonconformities, and management and certification issues. To ensure that the process proceeds according to the matrix, organizations must provide the registrar with requested information in a timely manner.

Annex 2. Criteria for Third-Party Auditor Qualification to ISO/TS 16949:2002

Auditors must follow ISO 19011:2000. There are qualifications, automotive industry-specific skills, minimum work experiences, and sanctioned automotive training rules that must be met by all auditors.

Annex 3. Audit Days for Certification to ISO/TS 16949:2002

Essentially, the total number of people in your organization determines the number of audit days that a registrar will need to spend at your organization. The IAOB Web site (*www.iaob.org*) clarifies this. The number of days allowed starts at two for an organization with fifteen employees and goes up to twenty-one days for an organization with more than 4,000 employees. You should discuss this with your registrar prior to signing any contracts for auditing.

If a corporate registration is being sought, an adjustment to the audit days can be based on the number of locations and the amount of duplicated information found at the individual sites.

Annex 4. Decertification Process to ISO/TS 16949:2002

Registrars must follow ISO/IEC Guide 62:1996 (or EN 45012), which explains the basics of how registrars should deal with auditees. This document gives additional rules that apply to the ISO/TS 16949:2002 process. A matrix is provided, giving the steps involved for decertification of a supplier to ISO/TS 16949:2002. With corporate certificates, if one site loses its registration, then the entire corporation also loses its registration.

SUMMARY

A careful reading of the rules document indicates that ISO/TS 16949:2002 requires more significant changes from registrars than it does from the suppliers being registered. The three documents released by the IATF are meant to assist the registrar and supplier in meeting ISO/TS 16949:2002's requirements. These manuals are to be used while performing an audit. IATF or IAOB members may periodically witness audit the uses of these manuals during registrar audits. If this should occur at your organization, you will be expected, and are required as part of your agreement to be audited to ISO/TS 16949:2002, to allow the witness auditors to view the audit process.

Chapter Fifteen

Customer-Specific Requirements

Many of ISO/TS 16949:2002's most important requirements are not in ISO/TS 16949:2002. The explanation for this seemingly contradictory statement is that all ISO/TS 16949 registrations must include verification that the supplier fully complies with the additional unique requirements of each of its customers that require ISO/TS 16949 registration. Unlike QS-9000, these requirements are not included in ISO/TS 16949. They are available from the customers and, in most cases, from the International Automotive Oversight Bureau (IAOB) Web site (*www.iaob.org*). Because the customer's requirements may modify or add to ISO/TS 16949's requirements, your organization's ISO/TS 16949 upgrade team should obtain these requirements as one of their first actions. You should check the IAOB Web site at least once a week, as changes occur regularly. (For example, Ford changed its information five times in the first year.)

A new set of sanctioned interpretations and frequently asked questions are being developed for ISO/TS 16949. These are called "The IATF-Adopted New Sanctioned Interpretation to ISO/TS 16949:2002 and FAQ." They can be found at *www.iaob.org*.

This chapter looks at the information available at the time of printing. However, it's extremely important to check the IAOB Web site regularly to ensure that you have the most current information available.

Some suppliers resent the idea of customer-specific requirements. More than one supplier representative has complained that ISO/TS 16949 is a failure because, like QS-9000 before it, there remain some requirements that have not been harmonized across the group of automakers subscribing to ISO/TS 16949. In reality, one requirement that applies to all automotive supplier companies could exist only in a perfect world. Some suppliers claim that they are different and that certain aspects of the

Figure 15.1—U.S. Automotive Core Tools

- 1990—Measurement System Analysis
- 1992—Statistical Process Control
- 1993—Production Part Approval Process
- 1993—Failure Mode and Effects Analysis
- 1994—Advanced Product Quality Planning/CP
- 1995—PPAP 2nd Ed., FMEA 2nd Ed. and MSA 2nd Ed.
- 1999—PPAP 3rd Ed.
- 2001—FMEA 3rd Ed.
- 2002—MSA 3rd Ed.

requirements don't apply to them. It is for this reason that the sanctioned interpretations have been created for ISO/TS 16949:2002.

CUSTOMER-SPECIFIC REQUIREMENTS

Because these requirements are updated on a regular basis, only the highlights are given here.

DaimlerChrysler (Chrysler Group)—September 2003

- Record retention of all PPAP-related documentation is required for the life of the part (production and service life), plus one year.
- Special characteristics go beyond those items identified in print. See DaimlerChrysler engineering standards for details.
- Design changes must be approved in writing.
- The PPAP manual must be used.
- A "needs improvement" notice to your organization must be reported in writing to your registrar within five days of receipt.
- QS-9000 will not be accepted after July 1, 2004.
- DaimlerChrysler's product assurance planning (PAP) will be used in conjunction with the supplier's APQP process.
- DaimlerChrysler requires a complete annual layout inspection for all parts (including subcomponents).

■ DaimlerChrysler's product assurance testing will be used for design verification (DV) and production validation (PV).

■ Internal audits must be done annually, at the minimum.

■ The DaimlerChrysler 7-Step Corrective Action Process must be used.

■ Continuing conformance inspection/tests shall be performed during the model year to ensure production items or products continue to meet specified requirements and tolerances.

■ An organization must have at each of its locations at least two individuals who have completed all DaimlerChrysler Corp. PRISM training.

■ Control plans are required for prototype, pre-launch, and production phases.

■ Suppliers must use the Global Supplier Portal electronic communications systems at *http://daimlerchrysler.covisint.com.*

Ford Motor Co.—October 2003

■ All suppliers must be registered to ISO/TS 16949:2002 by December 14, 2004. Additional details are provided in Q1 (see *https://web.bli.ford.com*).

■ Ford Engineering Standards may be obtained from Information Handling Services (800) 716-3447, or Autoweb Communications Inc., (616) 396-0880.

■ PPAP records (including purchase orders/amendments) will be maintained for the active life of the part, plus one calendar year.

■ Q1 continuous improvement requirements are to be met. Management review input must also include the Q1 2002 manufacturing site assessment results. The organization shall use the QOS assessment in the development of its QOS. The QOS Assessment is available online at *https://web.bli.ford.com.*

■ Ford Supplier Technical Assurance (STA) Engineer is to be contacted for changes to the manufacturing processes at the plant site

■ Unless otherwise approved by STA, the organization must ensure that only trained and qualified personnel are involved in all aspects of the manufacture or design (as appropriate) of Ford Motor Co. parts.

■ The organization must have evidence of lean manufacturing implementation plans as defined in the Q1 Manufacturing Site Assessment (found at *https://web.tcm.ford.com*).

■ Part dunnage is to be included in the requirements for cleanliness.

■ During the supplier's use of APQP, the Ford APQP reporting guidelines and forms must be reported (available online at *https://web.bli.ford.com*). Percent inspection points that satisfy tolerance (PIST) and percent indices that are process capable (PIPC) are part of these reports, if required by STA.

- Acceptance criteria for samples must be zero defects.

- Manufacturing feasibility reviews must be part of the APQP process.

- Multidisciplinary teams must be used in creating all FMEAs and control plans. (FMEAs are a high focus for Ford.)

- Material analysis, laboratory requirements, and lot traceability are to be reviewed.

- Ford uses the designation of special and critical characteristics for highlighted items.

- The Ford Product Development System (FPDS) must be used as outlined online at *https://fsn.ford.com/pd.frames.html.*

- The supplier must verify the design and development of its parts and that of all subcontractors.

- PPAP is to be used at all tiers of subcontractors. Run-at-rate will be established. The Ford Worldwide Engineering Release System (WERS) must be used and monitored.

- Subcontractor development can include registration or an STA-approved second-party auditor.

- Incoming quality metrics must be established and monitored as per the Q1 manufacturing site assessment requirements.

- All work done in the plant must be to the latest level of production.

- A documented system for preventive maintenance must be used. Top management must review the preventive maintenance system, and records must be maintained for one year after their creation.

- Logistical requirements include compliance to Material Management Operation Guideline (MMOG), Odette, or MS-9000, as specified by regional requirements.

- Set-up verification requirements include manual tooling exchanges. Records of all set-up verifications must be maintained for one year.

- All gages used for checking Ford components/parts as according to the control plan must have a gage reproducibility and repeatability (GR&R) test performed in accordance with the appropriate methods described by the latest AIAG *Measurement Systems Analysis* (MSA) manual to determine measurement capability. (Note that this means using "K" values aligned with Six Sigma.)

- If Ford places a plant on "Q1 Revocation," the supplier must contact its registrar in writing within five working days.

- Internal quality management system auditors shall be qualified per the outline provided (see chapter 16).
- Ongoing monitoring of process characteristics must be maintained. Suppliers must meet the engineering specification (ES) test performance requirements.
- A layout inspection and functional verification (to all engineering material and performance requirements) must be performed annually.
- Suppliers must prevent the delivery of nonconforming product. Use of quality rejects (QRs) and Global 8 Discipline Problem Solving (G8D) will be utilized.
- The supplier request for engineering approval (SREA) process must be used to request any waivers to the process and production.
- The International Automotive Task Force (IATF) documents for rules, guidance, and checklist will be used by the supplier.

General Motors—September 2002

- All records must be maintained during the production and service requirements, plus one calendar year.
- Electronic communication with GM's North American Operations must be maintained.
- The supplier must use GM's Key Characteristic Designation System definitions and symbols.
- All design changes must be made through written communication with the customer.
- PPAP must be utilized for all production parts.
- Trends in quality system performance and customer satisfaction should be compared to those of competitors, or appropriate benchmarks, and reviewed by top management.
- Internal auditors must be qualified as recommended in ISO 19011 and be knowledgeable in the process approach to auditing and in the five core tools manuals.
- Supplier development must be followed as outlined in ISO/TS 16949 and as listed in the GM customer-specific requirement. Written decision criteria must be established for the handling of small suppliers that do not have the resources to comply with a full ISO/TS 16949 audit process.
- Suppliers already registered to QS-9000 are acceptable until December 15, 2006. Otherwise, registration to ISO/TS 16949:2002 is required by December 15, 2004.

■ GM suppliers must verify annually that they are using the current version of these documents:

❑ Pre-Production/Pilot Material Shipping Procedures (GM 1407).

❑ Supplier Submission of Match Check Material (GM 1689).

❑ Shipping Parts Identification Label Standard (GM 1724).

❑ Component Verification & Traceability Procedure (GM 1730).

❑ Traceability Identifier Equipment (TIR 15-300) (GM 1731).

❑ Specifications for Part and Component Bar Codes ECV/VCVS (GM 1737).

❑ Supplier Quality Processes and Measurements Procedure (GM 1746).

❑ Continuous Improvement Procedure (GM 1747).

❑ GP-10 Evaluation and Accreditation Test Facilities (GM 1796/A).

❑ Shipping and Delivery Performance Requirements (GM 1797).

❑ Key Characteristics Designation System (KCDS) (GM 1805 QN).

❑ General Procedure for Pre-Prototype and Prototype Material (GM 1820).

❑ C4 Technology Program, GM—Supplier C4 Information (GM 1825).

❑ GP-12 Early Production Containment Procedure (GM 1920).

❑ Run at Rate Procedure (GM 1960).

(Note: Access the GM SupplyPower Web site for the current document version.)

■ GM Service Parts Operations (SPO) requires use of UPC labeling for certain commercial applications rather than AIAG labeling. Contact your SPO buyer for instructions.

■ If GM puts a supplier on "New Business Hold—Quality," the supplier must notify its registrar and an immediate probation period will be started.

■ Top management must review the quality system performance at planned intervals, but not less than annually.

THE IATF-ADOPTED NEW SANCTIONED INTERPRETATION TO ISO/TS 16949:2002

At the printing of this book, only a few clarifications are listed in the sanctioned interpretation. The first involves the use of the checklist to ISO/TS 16949 and the fact that auditors (internal and external) are to use it. In conjunction with this, once a supplier has been certified, if at any time following an audit a registrar identifies even a minor open issue, then the process of decertification is to begin.

At the end of an external audit, there must be no open issues (major or minor) at the supplier site. This rule is rigorously enforced by the IATF, and IOAB representatives have the right to witness audits by registrars without prior notice. Your company is required to allow an IOAB or IATF representative access to your facility to witness audits in progress at any time, with or without prior warning.

The second sanctioned interpretation clarification involves the number of audit days allowed for a specific site audit. In some cases, the number of days can be reduced, but limits are placed on how many days will be allowed, given the number of personnel working at the site.

If one site loses its certification, the certification for the entire company will be removed. For this reason, using the internal auditor process (see chapter 16) is critical to ensure that top management is aware of all issues that need to be addressed.

FREQUENTLY ASKED QUESTIONS (FAQ)
(AS OF JULY 24, 2003)

Q: Which organizations can obtain registration to ISO/TS 16949:2002?

A: Automotive suppliers sites that are making valued-added components for the automotive, truck (light, medium, or heavy), or motorcycle OEMs.

Q: What are the requirements for supplier development clause 7.4.1.2?

A: To understand your supplier development, you must look at both the standard and the IATF guidance documents. Essentially, if you want to do anything other than what is stated, you must have customer approval. If your supplier provides components that go to more than one of your customers, you need the approval of all customers who receive those parts.

At a minimum, ISO/TS 16949 requires having your suppliers in conformance (this isn't necessarily registration) with ISO 9001:2000 as the first step. (Remember that ISO 9001:1994 expired on December 15, 2003.) Once your suppliers are in conformance with ISO 9001:2000, your company is to work with them in conformance to ISO/TS 16949. It's expected that your plan will be completed within your first three years of registration to ISO/TS 16949 and that all of your suppliers will then be capable of becoming registered to ISO/TS 16949.

The IATF guidance documents give the sequence as:

1. Conformity with ISO 9001:2000
2. Achievement of ISO 9001:2000 registration as a minimum, unless otherwise specified by the customer
3. Compliance with ISO/TS 16949:2002, unless otherwise specified by the customer
4. Evidence of a process intended to achieve the previous three steps

Q: What is the correct way to calculate audit days, covering supporting functions for site and corporate certificates?

A: This question is related to external audits only and its answer is based on the number of employees in your company. The IATF wants registrars to spend a minimum of time with each supplier so they can acquire an understanding of what that supplier is doing in relationship to the ISO/TS 16949 requirements. Your registrar will work with you to help interpret this requirement for your particular situation.

Internal audits are a different situation. Top management in your organization must plan enough internal audit time to help ensure that all aspects of the organization are thoroughly covered. Remember that this is to be a value-adding activity, not a cops-and-robbers event. Internal auditors should be generating ideas for areas to improve in and should be writing many more preventive action requests that corrective action requests. The goal of the internal audit program should be to have looked at everything so well that the external auditors won't find even a minor issue.

Q: In addition to the ISO/TS 16949:2002 requirements document, are there additional reference manuals we should use?

A: The IATF manuals for rules, guidance, and the checklist (found in chapter 14) as well as the APQP, PPAP, FMEA, SPC, and MSA manuals (found in chapters 9 through 13, respectively) will be needed. Also, the various customer-specific requirements list company-specific manuals, as well as the IAOB Web site, which has the "IATF-Adopted New Sanctioned Interpretation of ISO/TS 16949:2002 and FAQ."

Customers may from time to time add requirements from various other sources (e.g., Ford's Q1 award program) that will have to be addressed by your organization.

Q: How can a site working toward ISO/TS 16949:2002 show twelve months of performance data?

A: Given a plant that has been in production for any length of time, this information should be readily available. Because ISO/TS 16949:2002 was released in March of 2002, it's expected that every plant has had well over a year to refine its customer data-collection methods. Top management has the responsibility to ensure that this information is being collected.

Q: For corporate situations where all the remote/support locations cannot be audited within the 90-day ISO/TS 16949:2002 requirement, may the audit timing be adjusted?

A: The IAOB will work with your registrar on a case-by-case basis to make a decision on the best course of action and issue a waiver, if appropriate.

SUMMARY

The overall process of ISO/TS 16949:2002 is a lot more stringent than either that of QS-9000 or ISO/TS 16949:1999 because many OEMs felt that those earlier requirements simply didn't provide the excellence needed in today's automotive industry. Another interesting factor was that every company had its own particular way that it wanted to run its business and so had slightly different needs and/or focuses that it expected from its suppliers. In the United States, for many years the fear of anti-monopoly legislation has trained the larger companies to be careful how they work together. This fear is still real in the automotive industry today. Accordingly, the reality of any communizing effort in the standards (quality, environmental, or health and safety) will result in each company asking for some things in slightly different ways.

Chapter Sixteen

Internal Auditing

T he automotive industry requires its suppliers to use internal auditors to verify their quality and environmental management systems (QMS and EMS) as outlined in ISO 9001:2000 and ISO 14001, respectively. However, the International Automotive Task Force (IATF) and Ford Motor Co. have directed additional training and experience above the general requirements of ISO 9001:2000. This chapter will discuss some of the qualifications of internal auditors and the process approach to auditing required in the automotive industry.

The controlling document used by the International Organization for Standardization (ISO) for auditing both QMSs and EMSs is *ISO 19011:2002 Guidelines for quality and for environmental management systems auditing.* This document is to be used by all organizations (registrars and companies seeking registration) to manage their auditing programs. Both ISO 9001:2000 and ISO/TS 16949:2002 require that top management conduct an internal audit program to ensure that management's planned results and customer satisfaction requirements are being met.

INTERNAL AUDITOR SELECTION

Top management is responsible for ensuring that internal auditors are adding value to the organization through the auditing process. Instead of good traffic cops—those who can read procedures and catch people doing something wrong—what is needed are individuals who will be able to look at processes from a systematic viewpoint and then generate ideas for improving customer satisfaction.

The organization should use ISO 19011:2002 as a guide when selecting internal auditors. ISO 19011 contains four clauses that auditors need to pay special attention to:

■ *Clause 4, Principles of audit program.* Internal auditors need to be ethical, able to provide fair (that is, appropriate) assessments, able to demonstrate a level of professionalism as defined by management, independent of the work that they normally do, and trained in the evidence-based process approach to auditing.

■ *Clause 5, Managing an audit program.* The audit program must be managed with identified objectives and goals. Some considerations for these could include management priorities, commercial intentions, management system requirements, governmental regulations, customer requirements, the need of other interested parties, and risks to the organization. Responsibilities, resources, and procedures for the audit program must be clearly defined and implemented, with records maintained, reviewed, and acted upon accordingly (as noted in clauses 5.2.1, 5.2.2, 5.3.1, 5.3.2, 5.3.3, 5.4, 5.5, and 5.6).

■ *Clause 6, Audit activities.* The audit process should follow a clearly defined process and apply all the basics of good auditing practice and technique (as flowcharted and outlined in ISO 19011). This typically starts with appointing the audit team leader; defining the audit objectives, scope, and criteria; determining the feasibility of the audit; selecting the audit team, and contacting the auditee. A document review should then be conducted, as well as preparation for the on-site audit activities. The standard on-site audit consists of an opening meeting, communication during the audit, establishing the roles and responsibilities of guides and observers, collecting and verifying information, generating audit findings, preparing audit conclusions, and conducting the closing meeting. An audit report is then prepared, and approvals and distribution take place according to plans. At this point the audit can be considered closed and follow-up procedures should be used to close any remaining open items.

■ *Clause 7, Competence and evaluation of auditors.* The organization must choose internal auditors who are competent in conducting internal audits. Important considerations are such personal attributes as knowledge and skills, education, work experience, auditor training and auditor experience, and maintenance and improvement of competence.

INTERNAL AUDITOR TRAINING

Your internal auditors will need training on ISO/TS 16949:2002. The internal auditors should start by reading all of ISO/TS 16949:2002 and the related core tool documents. There are a number of additional materials that are customer-specific which may need to be read, depending upon who your customers are (see chapter 11). Your organization should assign an individual to monitor customer-specific and general document updates and this person should confirm that internal auditors are being trained with the most current documents. For ISO/TS 16949:2002 and customer-specific requirements, visit *www.iaob.org* (this site should be checked weekly). The core tools and related documents can be found at *www.aiag.org*. For customer's documents, contact the customer's purchasing department.

Ford's customer-specific requirements have the strictest internal auditor procedure, and have been suggested as a potential automotive industry benchmark. Consider using the following outline to train/upgrade internal auditors in your organization:

■ An initial assessment of the understanding and ability to utilize the following documents, followed by formal training (usually a one-day minimum):
  ❑ The technical specification (ISO/TS 16949:2002)
  ❑ Related core tools (e.g., APQP, PPAP, FMEA, SPC, and MSA)
  ❑ Applicable customer-specific requirements
  ❑ The process approach to auditing

■ Ongoing testing and training in understanding and applying the following requirements:
  ❑ The technical specification (ISO/TS 16949:2002)
  ❑ Related core tools (e.g., APQP, PPAP, FMEA, SPC, and MSA)
  ❑ Applicable customer-specific requirements
  ❑ The process approach to auditing

■ Practice sessions (equivalent to one audit day) on:
  ❑ Case study audits
  ❑ Auditing role plays/simulations
  ❑ On-site audits

TURTLE DIAGRAM

The starting point for ISO/TS 16949 is to understand your organization's existing processes. Under QS-9000, many people came to understand the basic process model (see figure 16.1). This model can be seen in any activity and represents a

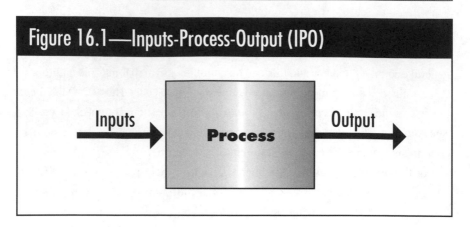

Figure 16.1—Inputs-Process-Output (IPO)

balance of energy going into a process and coming out. If you don't have a balance, waste is present in the process.

By understanding the basics of any activity through the process model, you can start looking deeper into what is happening in your organization. Six Sigma practitioners have expanded the process model to get the supplier-input-process-output-customer (SIPOC) model (see figure 16.2). This includes recognition that every process has customer(s) and supplier(s). Sometimes organizations change and processes that were at one time important are now no longer needed. The challenge is to determine if your current processes still add value to your organization and its customers.

Under ISO/TS 16949:2002, we now move to what is called the turtle diagram (see figure 16.3) for individual processes. This takes the basics of the process model

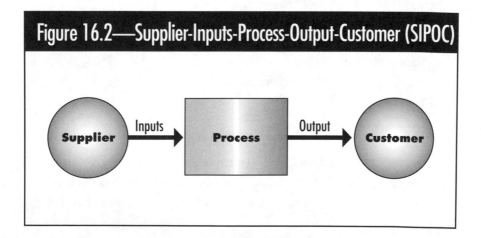

Figure 16.2—Supplier-Inputs-Process-Output-Customer (SIPOC)

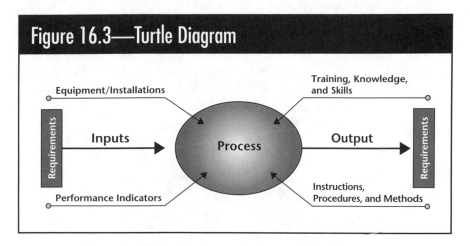

Figure 16.3—Turtle Diagram

Equipment/Installations

Training, Knowledge, and Skills

Requirements

Inputs

Process

Output

Requirements

Performance Indicators

Instructions, Procedures, and Methods

and adds aspects of the SIPOC to what is actually being done in the process to satisfy customers. Internal auditors must review these diagrams for every major process in your organization. If the internal auditors don't find such diagrams, they will have to create them as they go (remember to leave a copy in the area for the next auditor). Some say that the turtle diagram is a cross between the SIPOC and a cause-and-effect diagram. This is a good analogy because the turtle diagram looks at how the process satisfies the customer (typically an internal customer at this stage). By looking at what is really happening vs. what procedures say is supposed to be happening, an evaluation can be made as to whether the process is effective in meeting the customer's requirements.

OCTOPUS DIAGRAM

The next step is for management to start connecting the turtle diagrams (individual processes) into larger flow maps of how the company functions. This is called the octopus diagram (see figure 16.4) and it looks at the sequence of activities and how things actually work together. Top management may actually need several levels of maps to show high-level, medium-level, and shop/office activities. It's important to show how activities are interconnected and what is being done to satisfy the ultimate customers of your products and services. Internal auditors should evaluate the organization using the octopus diagram(s) to look for opportunities to improve customer satisfaction.

An analogy here could be the advanced product quality planning (APQP) process that was discussed earlier. Note that every output of one phase becomes an input

Figure 16.4—Octopus Diagram

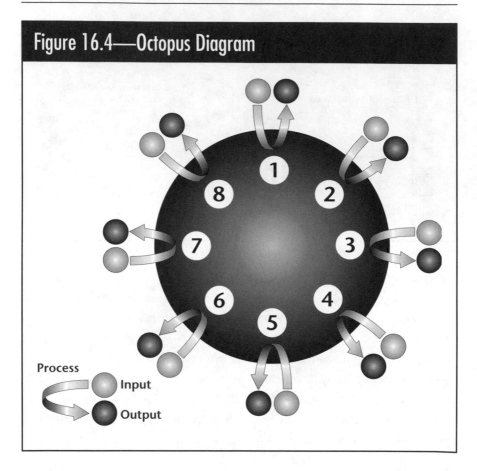

into the next phase of the planning model. Everything is used (a balanced system), thus making everything a valued-adding process. Waste is eliminated, and planning for contingencies is part of the process. This ensures that customers receive what they expect and what will work with their systems.

The organization should coordinate the construction of the octopus diagram, and evidence of the use of these diagrams might well appear in minutes of management meetings. Points (sometimes called process characteristics) that the organization should recognize in the processes include:

■ A process owner exists.
■ The process is defined.
■ The process is usually documented.
■ The process linkages are established.

Figure 16.5—Customer-Oriented Process—COP

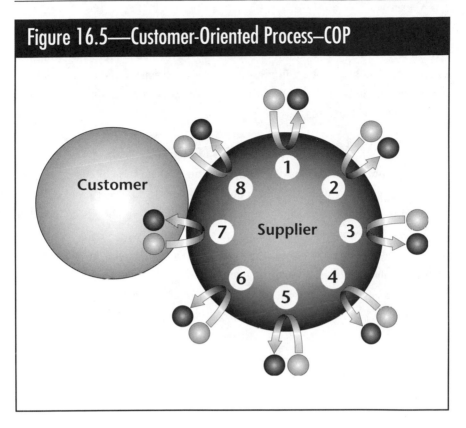

- The process is monitored.
- Records are maintained.

An organization can demonstrate full coverage of the QMS by using the octopus diagram as a guide/model for managing the organization. Reviews of what is actually occurring should be evident, and the use of the internal auditor reports become a key management tool in verifying that what is believed to be happening is in fact a reality. Some questions that can be asked during reviews are:

- If the process is eliminated, will the customer notice?
- Does the customer have a metric for the process?
- Do any of the inputs and/or outputs directly affect the customer?
- Have we identified the support processes as value-adding activities?
- If we were to design what we do from scratch, would it look that same as what we are doing today?

Internal auditors need to look for evidence that top management is asking these and other questions of the current systems. Such evidence is proof that continual improvement is being sought in every aspect of the business. (Note: In any given audit, internal auditors should be writing far more preventive action requests than corrective action requests.)

CUSTOMER-ORIENTED PROCESS

At any point in the octopus diagram, there can be some form of customer interface, either with an input and output, or both (see figure 16.5). These processes must be identified and given special attention to ensure that information is collected on customer satisfaction metrics.

■ These interaction points can include any number of activities. Some areas that the internal auditors can look for include:
■ Market analysis
■ Bid/tender
■ Order/request
■ Product and process design
■ Product and process verification/validation
■ PPAP
■ Product production
■ SQA/STA reviews
■ Shipping/delivery
■ Payment
■ Warranty/service
■ Post sales/customer feedback

One key point is to gather some type of customer input in these highlighted processes so that data are collected on what the customer perceives as value-adding activities. A correlation should then be established with the rest of the processes to ensure that what the company is doing is what will satisfy its customers. The internal auditors should look for this information and make a judgment as to how effective the overall process is in satisfying the customer.

PROCESS AUDITING

Here the evolution from QS-9000 and ISO/TS 16949:1999 to ISO/TS 16949:2002 can be seen. In ISO/TS 16949:2002, we start with what the customers say they want and need, and evaluate how the organization meets customer requirements. Internal auditors are tasked with reviewing the system, not the departments or functions as was required by QS-9000 or ISO/TS 16949:1999, from the standpoint of process effectiveness.

Establishing procedures and proving they are being followed will no longer suffice. Although that practice theoretically helps reduce variation for the customer, in actual practice it has been shown that after the auditors leave, organizations frequently go back to doing what they did before. Such behavior doesn't help the organization improve. Auditors are now to start by looking at the process effectiveness in all areas they visit, and to ask questions relating to customer wants and needs, and how those are being met.

Under ISO/TS 16949:2002 and ISO 9001:2000, auditors (internal and external) view the organization horizontally, according to the process model, instead of as a group of vertical/function departments. Customers see the results of the organization's work, so an ISO/TS 16949 audit will view the organization in the same manner. What is shown to auditors is merely what is done every day. This method requires top management to be much more involved in overseeing the QMS and more aware of the audit process than ever before. What is the organization, as a whole, doing to satisfy customers, and are plan's successes being evaluated in terms of the measurement of customer satisfaction?

SUMMARY

The internal auditing function under ISO/TS 16949:2002 covers a number of areas that were not addressed in QS-9000. The organization, including the management committee (instead of the management representative), has the responsibility to ensure that all aspects of the internal audit process are being planned, implemented, maintained, and that the information generated from the internal audit reports is being reviewed and acted upon during management meetings. If this is not the case, suboptimized results may be achieved and top management may miss opportunities for improving customer satisfaction.

The internal audit program must be seen as a value-adding activity for the organization. Top management must understand the reasons for taking people away from their regular jobs to review the overall system. This is why internal auditor selection is important and must be considered carefully. If the organization seriously considers the internal audit results and takes action appropriately, it can become an honor for employees to be asked to become internal auditors.

Chapter Seventeen

Management Review

Management review is the second and most important half of a powerful feedback loop. Suppliers who understand this concept and utilize it will achieve significant gains in productivity, quality, and customer satisfaction. Those who don't will get little from their ISO/TS 16949 registration beyond a certificate and the provisional opportunity to continue in the automotive supply base. Top management must conduct an analysis of your organization and make a decision as to which route they plan to take. Here, failing to plan is the same as planning not to achieve optimum performance. As W. Edwards Deming was fond of saying, employees work in the system; management works on the system.

Management review, quite simply, is the tool that management uses to work on the system.

Most knowledgeable people agree that management review was the least understood and most poorly implemented requirement of QS-9000. In fact, the requirement for management review in QS-9000 was both weak and nonspecific enough to be made trivial by suppliers who wished to do so. Many managers simply viewed management review as a task or assignment to tick off their to-do list. Little attention was given to seeing what areas of the organization needed improvement.

ISO/TS 16949 strongly nudges suppliers in the right direction by requiring not only evaluation of the "suitability, adequacy, and effectiveness" of the QMS but also the determination of opportunities for improvement (clause 5.6.1). More important, for the first time the inputs required for meaningful management review (clause 5.6.2) and the necessary outputs (clause 5.6.3) are specified. To get an idea of the potential of this, the inputs and outputs must be discussed in detail.

INPUTS

■ *Results of audits.* As we know from clause 8.2.2, ISO/TS 16949 defines three types of internal audits. In addition to these types, there are audits by the third-party registrar and customer audits (e.g., the Ford Q1 assessment). Data from all of these audits must be included in the management review at the first opportunity. These data must include not only the number of audits conducted but also their findings:

❑ What nonconformances were found?

❑ What was the cause of each nonconformance?

  ● Lack of training?

  ● Lack of proper equipment?

  ● Personnel issues?

  ● A better process was found?

❑ What corrective action was implemented?

❑ Has the effectiveness of the corrective action been verified?

❑ Were opportunities for improvement identified?

■ *Customer feedback.* The most basic type of customer feedback is the online data provided by the automakers and some tier-one suppliers. Additional feedback may be provided by the customer's rejection of incoming product, formal problem reports, or supplier initiatives to determine customer satisfaction (clause 8.2.1).

■ *Process performance and product conformity.* This is a generic heading for the metrics used to monitor processes. Trend charts with identification of significant events (e.g., nonconforming raw material, operator error) are normally the best way to present these data. To help identify changes in the processes, these data should be compared with historical data.

■ *Status of corrective and preventive actions.* For all customer and internally identified problems, status must be provided using the customer-required format (e.g., 8D, 7D, PR&R).

■ *Follow-up actions from previous management reviews.* The status of all assignments from the preceding management review must be presented. If an assignment is to be closed, appropriate evidence of the effectiveness of the action must be provided.

■ *Changes that could affect the quality management system.* Potential effects could result from volume or shift pattern changes, new model products, new sources of production materials (e.g., plastic resin, purchased piece parts), or nonproduction materials (e.g., welding electrodes, cutting fluids, drill bits). An FMEA should be conducted for such changes and the failure modes with high risk priority numbers presented, along with the actions planned for eliminating or reducing the effect of each.

■ *Recommendations for improvement.* These recommendations, and the actions resulting from them, are the pay-off and justification for management review. If no actions result from the management review, it seems obvious that time was wasted. Incidentally, a nonconformance to ISO/TS 16949 has also occurred.

■ *Analysis of actual and potential field failures.* Suppliers whose products fail in the field are responsible for analyzing the returned parts and for determining not only corrective actions but also including the quality, safety, and environmental implications of the failures in management review.

Planning and Conducting the Meeting

Agendas that include all of the inputs that are applicable to the supplier must be developed for management review meetings. During such meetings, the data from each input should be presented using simple statistical tools such as Pareto charts and trend charts. Improving or deteriorating trends should be flagged. Wherever possible, proposals for improvement actions should be presented in a form that will lead to a decision during the meeting. Target dates and verification methods for such actions should be determined.

OUTPUTS

■ *QMS improvements.* If changes to the QMS will improve its effectiveness, the specific QMS process to be improved must be identified and the responsibility for the change assigned to an appropriate person. If more than one functional department is affected, it may be necessary to convene an ad hoc team to determine the optimum solution. If the documented procedure for the process was originally developed by a team, that team should be reconvened to address improving the process. The output of a QMS improvement frequently will be an improved procedure.

- *Product improvements.* If the product doesn't conform to specifications, it is necessary to identify the production operation causing the nonconformity. Statistical analysis of process capability may be required. If the product meets all customer specifications and is still causing problems, design engineering should meet with the customer to learn what new product requirements are necessary.
- *Additional resources.* When it is determined that some sort of additional resources are required to improve a situation, the management review output must indicate what these resources are, how they will be obtained, and by whom, with appropriate target dates.

For all actions that are directed during a management review meeting, it's important to determine how verification of the assigned action will occur. Data from internal processes or from the customer can be plotted on the statistical charts that were originally used to identify the issue.

The size of the supplier, the complexity of its processes, and the number and significance of quality issues (e.g., customer complaints, scrap, rework, and warranty expense) will determine the frequency of management review meetings. In a plastics molding plant with a hundred employees and a parts per million defect rate (ppm) at the customer of less than 50, a management review meeting every six months is appropriate. In a more complex plant, with several hundred employees, more complex products, and a ppm level of more than 50, a management review should occur at least quarterly, or even monthly. Note that there need not be a separate meeting specifically for management review. As long as the necessary inputs are considered and appropriate outputs result from the meeting, management review can be incorporated in a regularly scheduled operations review, if the supplier is already using that approach.

On a final note, remember that suppliers who schedule the management review immediately before the surveillance assessment by their registrar reinforce the idea that the management review happens only to satisfy the auditor. Management review should be scheduled on a regular basis, whether monthly, quarterly, or twice per year, and at natural times, such as the end of a quarter. Management review must be integrated into the company's culture, making it a normal part of doing business.

The bottom line is effectiveness. Does management review result in actions that improve quality, productivity, and customer satisfaction? If so, the intent (continuous improvement), of clause 8.3, and more important, of clause 8.5.1, is being met.

SUMMARY

Top management must be focused on continually improving everything in the organization. One way of establishing this mindset is through a comprehensive management review process. This chapter has highlighted the standard and provided common-sense explanations of what managers should be doing. This is not about adding tasks to managers, but about how to convert what is already being done into a process of continual improvement for the organization.

POTENTIAL REQUESTS FROM YOUR AUDITOR

- Provide the inputs and outputs from the most recent management review
- Provide the status of assignments made in the management review
- Show what changes have been made to the QMS and to various processes as a result of the management review

Chapter Eighteen

Issues From ISO/TS 16949:2002 Registration Audits to Date

I n preparation for this book, we interviewed a number of registrar auditors and others to get a sampling of the issues found during registration to ISO/TS 16949:2002. By far the largest problem area is the shift from "clause-based" to "process-based" thinking. Many suppliers still view their task as incorporating specific actions to meet each of ISO/TS 16949:2002's requirements. This unfortunate and counterproductive approach stems directly from the way these companies approached QS-9000. Remember:

> *The most significant change in moving from QS-9000 or ISO/TS 16949:1999 to ISO/TS 16949:2002 is the process approach introduced in ISO 9001:2000.*

The solution to this problem is to use flowcharts to understand your company's processes. You must begin with these processes, not with ISO/TS 16949. If you understand your company's processes, and then determine how the requirements relate to your processes, you will be on the right track to successful ISO/TS 16949 registration *and* a more efficient organization.

A related problem is that the interactions between processes comprising the quality management system (QMS) often are not addressed in the quality manual and procedures. Again, the cause is a lack of "process thinking," a situation made worse when only one person is responsible for developing the QMS. The solution is to have the people who are part of the processes develop and review the flowcharts. This must be done for each process, and every function that has any involvement in the process must be represented.

In the same vein, problems frequently result from ineffective internal system audits. Such audits must begin with the flowcharts for the process, not with ISO/TS 16949:2002's requirements. System audit checklists must be developed from the flowcharts and then compared with the standard to determine if all requirements are being met. Read chapter 1 (Automotive Process-Oriented Approach Auditing) in the IATF Checklist to ISO/TS 16949:2002.

Specific nonconformances related to internal audits include:

■ ISO/TS 16949:2002 internal audit training had not been completed at the time of the audit—clause 8.2.2.5. (Inadequate internal auditor training is one of the top three failures found in ISO/TS 16949 registrations.)

■ Written findings did not have the required three elements—requirement, objective evidence, and nature of nonconformance—clause 8.2.2/ISO 10011 series guidance documents.

■ Management was never audited—clause 8.2.2.4.

■ The audit schedule did not include auditing of all QMS processes—clause 8.2.2.

■ Audit notes for process audits sampled did not clearly document auditing all processes—clause 8.2.2.

Top managers are frequently unfamiliar with their responsibilities (refer to ISO/TS 16949:2002 section 5) and look to the management representative to answer most or all of the auditor's questions. This behavior is not only a problem but also an immediate tip-off to your auditor that your company has not understood ISO/TS 16949's requirements. Auditors take the "top management shall…" statements of section 5 seriously. If the auditor finds any indication that your managers aren't familiar with, and meeting, their responsibilities, nonconformances will be issued. Section 5 provides plenty of opportunities for this.

Given the cursory nature of many suppliers' management review under QS-9000, it's not surprising that ISO/TS 16949's more rigorous management review requirements are frequently not met. Numerous nonconformances have been written for failure of the management review to address such required inputs as internal audit results, the status of internal audit corrective actions, and follow-up of actions from previous management reviews. Failure to address outputs, such as recommendations for improvements to the quality system, also generates nonconformances.

Other significant issues, arranged in order of the ISO/TS 16949 clause, are:

- Registration scheme rules are not followed—4.1
- The quality policy does not address continual improvement of the QMS—4.2/5.3
- Records are not linked to procedures—4.2.4
- The master design failure mode and effects analysis are ahead of the copy that is used by the employees (i.e., master is at rev. 19 and working copies are at rev. 18)—4.5.2.1
- The work instructions for maintenance identifies four types of equipment for a preventive maintenance (PM) schedule, but current practice is to only record PM for fork trucks. There is no evidence for the other three equipment types—4.9.1.5
- The work instruction for the label associate identifies tasks that are not currently performed by the label associate—4.9.2
- Competence of new candidates for operator positions is established by an outside firm. It's questionable whether these tests adequately assess competence for the skill sets needed for the position—6.2.2
- On-the-job training is not addressed—6.2.2.3
- A contingency plan has been developed for emergency situations; however, the plan does not clearly address satisfying customer requirements in the event of emergencies—6.3.2
- The contingency plan does not include specific recovery systems to deal with events that could affect meeting customer schedules (e.g., power outages, customer rejections, IT network breakdown, and facility/product damage by natural disasters)—6.3.2
- Unreported changes (production part approval process [PPAP])—7.1.4, 7.3.6.3
- Customer specifics are ignored—7.2.1, 7.2.1.1, 7.3.2.3
- Interface between site and remote location are not effective—7.3.1, 7.4.1 (and others)
- PPAP is not being followed or does not meet requirements—7.3.6.3/customer-specific section II of PPAP manual requirements.
- There is no evidence that measurements at specified stages of design and development are being reported as inputs to management review—7.3.4.1
- Control plans are superficial and/or are not being followed—7.5.1.1
- The manufacturing instructions do not identify the special characteristics defined on the process failure mode and effects analysis and control plan—7.5.1.2
- Records of operator set-up verification have not been completed—7.5.1.3

■ Many gages are past their calibration due dates. Status of gages used in decommissioning production lines is unknown—7.6

■ Gage repeatability and reproducibility (GR&R) tests are performed by calibration technicians, not by the people actually using the gages. Suppliers have their lab technicians do the GR&R on the tool/gage and then assign the tool/gage to an operator or inspector with only brief instruction—7.6/MSA manual requirements

■ The current ppm criteria is above what is required by customers—8.2.1, 8.2.1.1, 8.4, 5.2

■ An obsolete version of the MSA manual is being used (second edition instead of the third edition).

What do these nonconformances have in common? They all could have been identified by a thorough internal systems audit. Many of them portray an organization fixated on "getting registered," rather than creating a lean, effective QMS. There are three lessons to learn from this:

■ Take the time to develop a solid QMS that fits your company's business.

■ Conduct thorough system audits.

■ Correct the deficiencies.

Orient your company to view ISO/TS 16949:2002 registration as a report card for the organization, not as a goal to be reached, or a hurdle to be jumped. Registration to ISO/TS 16949:2002 can only be accomplished as a team effort. Attempts to make it the responsibility of a single person will likely fail.

Chapter Nineteen

Conclusion(s) and Beginning(s)

The main message of this book is that if your company benefits from the transition to ISO/TS 16949:2002, the benefits will come not from getting registered but from the way your company approaches getting registered. Registration is important but the certificate hanging on the wall adds no value to your company other than by qualifying you for future business.

Consider the history of the Japanese automotive industry. When their cars were first imported to the United States in the 1960s, their quality was terrible. However, every year there was a 3 to 5 percent improvement in quality. Then new models were launched, with 50 percent reductions in customer-reported problems. By 1984, Japanese and U.S. cars had roughly equivalent reliability. The 3 to 5 percent annual improvements continued, along with occasional revolutionary improvements in new models. The outcome of this progression was inevitable.

Despite such obvious examples, continuous improvement remains an unfamiliar idea to many suppliers. Maintaining the status quo is much closer to the way most managers view product creation and production processes. Quality is considered either "fixed" or "broken." This is a ridiculous way to view things. Today's quality is never good enough for tomorrow.

ISO/TS 16949:2002 is the voice of your customers, demanding that you have effective processes in place. The goal is consistent reliability. If your company is mature enough to understand that an investment in developing a robust QMS will yield significant benefits in the future, then gaining your ISO/TS 16949:2002 registration will be straightforward.

However, it is vital that your company's position on the following points is clear:

■ Top management must be involved in overseeing the ongoing development, management, and improvement of the QMS.

■ Development of the QMS can only be effective when done by a team (or teams). Your company's sales, engineering, production, and finance personnel must be actively involved in the development of the QMS.

■ Process thinking is key. Both process owners and participants from several functions must be involved in developing flowcharts that accurately reflect the organization's actual processes.

■ Documentation should be kept to the minimum necessary to meet the need. Procedures are necessary when there are interfaces between personnel, functional departments, and sites. These procedures should typically be one page in length and rarely more than two. Flowcharts should be integral to most, if not all, procedures.

■ There are three indicators of the health of your organization's QMS:
  ❑ Internal audit findings
  ❑ Management review outputs
  ❑ Customer satisfaction indicators

Any competent auditor, after spending ten minutes reviewing these data, will understand if your company is serious about quality or is merely trying to go through the motions to achieve registration.

■ If nonconformances are found during your registration audit, your company must not view them as failures but as opportunities for improvement.

■ Your QMS is the foundation of your business. Effectiveness is the goal. Improve, clarify, simplify, and never stop.

As long-time practitioners in quality improvement, we hope that this book is useful to your company, not merely in achieving ISO/TS 16949:2002 registration, but in developing a robust QMS that provides competitive advantage and a prosperous future.

IATF-Approved ISO/TS 16949 Registrars

As of Oct. 20, 2003, the following certification bodies are accredited by the International Automotive Task Force to certify/register suppliers to ISO/TS 16949:2002:

ABS-QE

ABS Quality Evaluation Inc.
6000 Lombardo Center Drive, Ste. 135
Cleveland, OH 44131
Tel: (216) 328-9220
Fax: (216) 328-9256
Internet: *www.abs-qe.com*

AENOR

Associación Española de
Normalización
CI GENOVA, 6
28004 Madrid
Spain
Tel: (34) 914-32-60 00
Fax: (34) 913-10-40-32
Internet: *www.aenor.es*

AFAQ

Association Française pour
l'Assurance de la Qualité
116 av Aristide Briand, BP 40
92224 Bagneux
France
Tel: (33) 1-46-11-38-39
Fax: (33) 1-46-11-39-60
Internet: *www.afaq.org*

AIB

AIB Vinçotte
157 Avenue du roi
1190 Bruxelles
Belgium
Tel: (32) 2-536-83-71
Fax: (32) 2-536-83-17
Internet: *www.aib-vincotte.com*

AQA

AQA International LLC
1105 Belleview Ave.
Columbia, SC 29201
Tel: (803) 779-8150
Fax: (803) 779-8109
Internet: *www.aqausa.com*

AQSR

AQSR International Inc.
3025 Boardwalk Drive, Ste. 120
Ann Arbor, MI 48108
Tel: (734) 913-8055
Fax: (734) 913-8152
Internet: *www.aqsr.com*

ASR

American Systems Registrar
4550 Cascade Road, Ste. 104
Grand Rapids, MI 49546
Tel: (888) 891-9022
Fax: (616) 942-6409
Internet: *www.asrworldwide.com*

BSI

British Standards Institution
389 Chiswick High Road
London W4 4AL
United Kingdom
Tel: 44 (0) 20-8996-9000
Fax: 44 (0) 20-8996-7400
Internet: *www.bsi-global.com*

BVQI

Bureau Veritas Quality International
2nd Floor, Tower Bridge Court
114-226 Tower Bridge Road
London SE1 2TX
United Kingdom
Tel: (44) 207-661-0700
Fax: (44 207-661-0700
Internet: *www.bvqi.com*

CERMET

CERMET Soc. Cons a r.l.
Sede Legale, Operativa e Direzione
Via Cadriano, 23
40057 Cadriano di Granarolo
Emilia (BO)
Italy
Tel: (39) 51-764-830
Fax: (39) 51-763-382
Internet: *www.cermet.it*

CERTO

CERTO S.r.l.
Corso Montevecchio 38
10129 Torino
Italy
Tel: (39) 011-5165700
Fax: (39) 011-5165777
Internet: *www.certo.it*

CISQ

CISQ Automotive (including CERTI-QUALITY, ICIM, IGQ, IIP, IMQ, and RINA)
Via Quintiliano 41

20138 Milano
Italy
Tel: (39) 02-502371
Fax: (39) 02-501196
Internet: *www.cisq.com*

CRS

CRS Registrars Inc.
135 Chesterfield Lane, Ste. 201
Maumee, OH 43537
Tel: (419) 861-1689
Fax: (419) 861-1696
Internet: *www.crsregistrars.com*

DEKRA

Dekra-ITS Certification Services
GmbH
Handwerkstrasse 15
70565 Stuttgart
Germany
Tel: (49) 711-7861-2906
Fax: (49) 711-7861-2615
Internet: *www.dekra-its.de*

DNV

Det Norske Veritas Certification
16340 Park Ten Place, Ste. 100
Houston, TX 77084-5143
Tel: (281) 721-6724
Fax: (281) 721-6903
Internet: *www.dnvcert.com*

DQS

DQS Deutsche Gesellschaft zur
Zertifizierung
August-Schanz-Strasse 21
60433 Frankfurt am Main
Germany
Tel: (49) 69-95427-189
Fax: (49) 69-95427-212
Internet: *www.dqs.de*

Eagle

Eagle Registrations Inc.
402 Kettering Tower
Dayton, OH 45423
Tel: (937) 223-3025
Fax: (937) 223-3927
Internet: *www.eagleregistrations.com*

Entela

Entela Inc. QSRD
2625 Buchanan S.W.
Grand Rapids, MI 49548-1206
Tel: (616) 222-7979
Fax: (616) 222-7999
Internet: *www.entela.com*

GCS-SABS

Global Conformity Services Ltd. -
SABS
1 Dr. Lategan Road Groenkloof
Private Bag X191
Pretoria 0001
South Africa
Tel: (27) 12-428-6405

Fax: (27) 12-428-6703
Internet: *www.sabs.co.za*

INTER Cert
International Cert Zertifizierung
GmbH
Straubinger Strasse 2
94333 Geiselhöring
Germany
Tel: (49) 9423-9412-0
Fax: (49) 9423-9412-50
Internet: *www.international-cert.de*

ITS-Intertek
ITS Intertek Testing Services
70 Codman Hill Road
Boxborough, MA 01719
Tel: (407) 474-4748
Fax: (407) 330-9078
Internet: *www.itsintertek.com*

JQA
Japan Quality Assurance Organization
Akasaka Twin Tower 4F
2-17-22 Akasaka
Minato-ku, Tokyo 107-0052
Japan
Tel: (81) 3-3584-9474
Fax: (81) 3-3224-9002
Internet: *www.jqa.jp*

KFQ
Korean Foundation for Quality
FKI Building, 28-1, Yoido-Dong
Youngdungpo-Gu

150-756 Seoul
Korea
Tel: (82) 2-767-4951
Fax: (82) 2-767-4990
Internet: *www.ksaqa.or.kr*

KPMG
KPMG Fides Peat Certification
Badenerstrasse 172
CH-8026 Zürich
Switzerland
Tel: (41) 01-249-46 33
Fax: (41) 01-249-25 5
Internet: *www.kpmg.com*

LGAI
LGAI Technological Center
Apartat de Correus 18
08193 Bellaterra (Barcelona)
Spain
Tel: (34) 93-567-20-00
Fax: (34) 93-567-20-01
Internet: *www.lgai.es*

LRQA
Lloyds Register Quality Assurance
Hiramford - Middlemarch Office
Village
Siskin Drive
Coventry CV3 4FJ
United Kingdom
Tel: (44) 24-7688-2222
Fax: (44) 24-7663-9493
Internet: *www.lrqa.com*

MQZ

Moody Q-Zert GmbH

Bleichstrasse 19

75173 Pforzheim

Germany

Tel: (49) 7231-929611

Fax: (49) 7231-929620

Internet: *http://qzert.de*

NIS ZERT

NIS Zertifizierungs- und

Umweltgutachter GmbH

Doernigheimer Strasse 2

63452 Hanau

Germany

Tel: (49) 6181-9937-15

Fax: (49) 6181-9937-84

Internet: *www.nis-zert.de*

NQA

National Quality Assurance Ltd.

Warwick House Houghton Hall Park,

Houghton Regis

Dunstable, Beds LU5 5ZX

United Kingdom

Tel: (44) 1582-539000

Fax: (44) 1582-539090

Internet: *www.nqa.com*

NSF

NSF International Strategic

Registrations Ltd.

789 N. Dixboro Road

Ann Arbor, MI 48105

Tel: (888) 673-9000

Fax: (734) 827-6801

Internet: *www.nsf-isr.org*

ÖQS

ÖQS - Zertifizierungs - und

Begutachstungs GmbH

Gonzagagasse 1/25

A-1010 Wien

Austria

Tel: (43) 1-533-30-50

Fax: (43) 1-533-30-50-9

Internet: *www.oeqs.com*

PSB

PSB Certification Pte Ltd.

3 Science Park Drive

No. 03-12 PSB Annex

Singapore 118 223

Tel: (65) 6885-1628

Fax: (65) 6872-0531

Internet: *www.psbcert.com*

QCB

Quality Certification Bureau

103, Advanced Technology Centre

9650, 20th Ave.

Edmonton, AB T6N 1G1

Canada

Tel: (780) 496-2463

Fax: (780) 496-2464

Internet: *www.qcbinc.com*

QMI

Quality Management Institute

90 Burnhamthorpe Road W., No. 300

Mississauga, ON L5B 3C3
Canada
Tel: (905) 272-3920
Fax: (905) 272-3942
Internet: *www.qmi.com*

RW TÜV

RW-TÜV Systems GmbH
Langemarckstrasse 20
45141 Essen
Germany
Tel: (49) 201-825-3317
Fax: (49) 201-825-3278
Internet: *www.rwtuev-at.de*

SAI

SAI Global Ltd.
286 Sussex St
Sydney, NSW 2000
Australia
Tel: (61) 2-8206-6060
Fax: (61) 2-8206-6001
Internet: *www.sai-global.com*

SGS

SGS-ICS Gesellschaft für
Zertifizierungen mbH und
Umweltgutachter
Raboisen 28
20095 Hamburg
Germany
Tel: (49) 40-30101-367
Fax: (49) 40-330408
Internet: *www.sgs.com*

SIRIM

SIRIM-QAS Sdn. Bhd.
Building 4, SIRIM Complete
1 Persiaran
Dato' Menteri
Shah Alam, Selangor 40911
Malaysia
Tel: (60) 3-5544-6359
Fax: (60) 3-5544-6487

Smithers

Smithers Quality Assessments Inc.
425 W. Market St.
Akron, OH 44303-2099
Tel: (330) 762-4231
Fax: (330) 762-7447
Internet: *www.smithersregistrar.com*

SQS

Schweiz. Vereinigung für Qualtäts-
und Management-Systeme
Bernstrasse 103
GH-3052 Zollikofen
Switzerland
Tel: (41) 31-910-3535
Fax: (41 31-910-3545
Internet: *www.sqs.ch*

SRI

SRI Quality System Registrar
105 Bradford Road, Ste. 400
Wexford, PA 15090
Tel: (724) 934-9000

Fax: (724) 935-6825
Internet: *www.sriregistrar.com*

TAT

TÜV Anlagentechnik
Am grauen Stein
51105 Köln
Germany
Tel: (49) 221-806-2287
Fax: (49) 221-806-1573
Internet: *www.tuev-rheinland.de*

TMS

TÜV Management Service GmbH
Ridlerstrasse 65
80339 München
Germany
Tel: (49) 89-5791-2504
Fax: (49) 89-5791-2192
Internet: *www.tuvglobal.com*

TÜV Hessen

TÜV Cert - Zertifizierungsstelle des
TÜV Hessen
Rüdesheimer Strasse 119
64285 Darmstadt
Germany
Tel: (49) 6151-600-331
Fax: (49) 6151-600-336
Internet: *www.tuev-hessen.de*

TÜV Nord

TÜV Nord Cert GmbH & Co. KG
Am TÜV 1
30519 Hannover

Germany
Tel: (49) 511-8380-500
Fax: (49) 511-8380-555
Internet: *www.tuev-nord.de*

TÜV Saar

TÜV Saarland e.V.
Am TÜV 1
66280 Sulzbach
Germany
Tel: (49) 6897-506-114
Fax: (49) 6897-506-228
Internet: *www.tuev-saar-cert.de*

UL

Underwriters Laboratories
1285 Walt Whitman Road
Melville, NY 11747-3081
Tel: (631) 271-6200
Fax: (631) 439-6030
Internet: *www.ul.com*

URS

United Registrar of Systems Ltd.
United House
Station Road
Cheddar
Somerset, BS27 3AH
United Kingdom
Tel: (44) 1934-743-999
Fax: (44) 1934-744-300
Internet: *www.urs.co.uk*

UTAC

Union Technique de l'Autombile et du
Cycle
Autodrome de Linas-Montlhéry
BP 212
91311 Montlhéry
France
Tel: (33) 1-69-80-17-00
Fax: (33) 1-69-80-17-17
Internet: *www.utac.com*

VCA

Vehicle Certification Agency
1 The Eastgate Office Centre
Eastgate Road
Bristol BS5 6XX
United Kingdom
Tel: (44) (0) 117-952-4161
Fax: (44) (0) 117-952-4146
Internet: *www.vca.gov.uk*

ZSQ

Zertifizierungsstelle für
Qualitätsmanagementsysteme des
Kraftfahrt-Bundesamtes
Postfach 12 01 53
01002 Dresden
Germany
Tel: (49) 351-473-85-23
Fax: (49) 351-473-85-36
Internet: *www.kba.de*

Index